This study contributes to deeper understanding of how self-interest creates economic inefficiency and is bad for economic development. The author, writing in clear, compelling language, comprehensively analyzes environments in developing countries where the greater part of the population is poor and miserable. Thus, this book is a must-read for every scholar interested in the socio-economic development of developing economies.

Ellis B. Beteck, Ph.D. International Affairs and Development

This book introduces a refreshing perspective to the discussion on the barriers to economic development in third world countries. It is one of the rare moments when the pursuit of self-interest by developed nations is held accountable for slow development in third world countries.

David Tataw, PhD, MMIS,MPA,FACHE

THE DIALECTIC OF ECONOMIC DEVELOPMENT

How the Logic of Self-Interest Impedes Progress

JOHN TATAW MANGA

CONTENTS

To my mother, Agnes Batembo Manga.

And to the memory of my father, Bernard Arrey Manga Besong.

ACKNOWLEDGMENTS

I wish to express my deep gratitude to Dr. Betek, to Dr. Ayuk Augustine Ayuk, and to my fellow Toastmaster Mr. John Grinder for accepting to read parts of this book and for offering suggestions, which have somehow made the book a better read.

Thanks especially to Evelyne M. Langer, my companion, for designing the cover page and for all the patience and encouragement, without which it would have been difficult to complete the writing of this book.

INTRODUCTION

The need to undertake this work on the obstacles to economic development first occurred to me some years ago. I had then just started studying political economy at college when, at a chance meeting with some industrialists and clergymen, I became engaged in a debate on the problems of the transfer of technology.

It dawned on me, for the first time perhaps, that through the control of technical knowledge and other important resources, the countries of the North were in a position to dictate the rhythm of development in the South. This was the conclusion I reached after one of the participants at the debate questioned the wisdom of transferring technology to the South. He said, "Isn't the transfer of technology or the sale of highly sophisticated capital goods to the South going to lead to the economic suicide of the North?"

To say the least, this is a very genuine preoccupation for anyone who owes his dominance over others to his control of knowledge and technology.

Prior to this meeting, I held the view shared by many in the Third World that all that the South needed to do was to imitate the North. Never had it occurred to me that efforts to imitate the developed countries could be hindered in any way. Seeing the machines and the methods of production that were in use in the First World and considering them easily transferable, I had even come to the hasty conclusion that the South should be able to make up for its economic backwardness in less than fifty years. Well, I took for granted the willingness of the North to *cooperate* in the development process. That was rather naïve of me.

This work is not about how certain countries became underdeveloped. It is rather about why they remain underdeveloped despite great achievements in science and technology in recent times. In other words, it is about one other factor—self-interest—that may be holding back development in the South.

A lot of literature already exists on this subject in which underdevelopment is blamed on several factors, including the lack of capital, the lack of entrepreneurship, the lack of appropriate technology, the lack of natural resources, or the existence of hostile climatic conditions. Underdevelopment is also blamed on the unfavorable political climate that exists in many Third World countries. Important as the contribution of those factors may be to development, do they sufficiently explain the continued state of underdevelopment in the South? Probably not; there might be more to it than just the lack of these resources.

In this work, I have tried to examine at least one other factor that may be contributing to the continued backwardness in the South: the attitude of the developed societies, which is dictated by self-interest concerns. Are they willing to have other Japans or other Chinas or other emerging economies mushrooming at their doorstep? If the answer to this question is no (which I truly believe it is), are they in a position to prevent such mushrooming? I dare to suggest that they might already be doing so without admitting it.

Some authors have refused to be realistic and have instead shown a naïve disregard for sociopolitical realities and for vested interests. Professor Hirschman's theory of *possibilism* is based on this naïve disregard. My own view is that there exists a subtle but nonetheless tremendous resistance to development. It stems neither from some unexplained love for underdevelopment nor from sadism but rather from the desire, which all people have, to defend their interests. It stems also from their eagerness to protect their privileged positions. This is even more so when we reckon that their control of economic and political powers is their only real guaranty of a continued high standard of living.

Contrary to what experts continue to assert, it is believed by many that, on balance, development in the South will threaten the North's social and material welfare. Of course, such threats do not even need to be real for people to adopt a defensive attitude. It suffices that they believe in its existence for them to take preemptive measures. This attitude is a force to be reckoned with in the planning of economic development.

To the pessimistic reader, the doubts I raise about the North's intentions of cooperating in the development of the South might sound rather fatalistic. My intention has been, on the contrary, to alert readers to the dangers of placing confidence in outsiders to do one's tasks for one. Assistance of any kind—based on the doctrine of mutual dependence—is no more than a farce. If, as former US secretary of state Gen. Colin L. Powell stated in an article in *Foreign Policy* magazine, "foreign aid that succeeds is foreign aid that makes itself obsolete," then all genuine assistance, with long-term positive effects to the recipient, is self-defeating (from the point of view of the donor) in that it tends to remove the power gap between the donor and the recipient. In other words, it sharpens the competition between them as the dependence of the one on the other is reduced.

Although most, if not all, of my examples are drawn from situations in the North-West/South relations, this work is not to be seen as an attack on the capitalist system. As the anecdote below shows, I have the strong conviction that socialist countries (if they still existed in reality) would adopt a similar attitude when confronted with a similar situation. The anecdote goes to suggest one thing—that a lot more might be running on self-interest than we are willing to admit.

At a book fair recently, I stopped at a stand to discuss with the lady in attendance. In the course of our brief conversation, I let her know that I was researching the reasons why countries of the South may never be developed. Then she inquired, "Under capitalism?"

"No," I said, "it doesn't matter whether it is under capitalism or under communism. The relationship between the developed countries and the underdeveloped countries remains the same irrespective of the political system involved."

"It is under capitalism that the South may never develop," she insisted.

"Well," I said, "when Communist Soviet Union was still around, they did not cater very much to the interests of the South. Instead, they were concerned only with their own interests."

"The Soviet Union was not really practicing communism," she said. "What they practiced was Stalinism, and they did not care very much about other countries."

"That is the point I'm trying to make," I said. "It is that desire to pursue one's own interests to the detriment of those of others that affects the relationship between the North and the South, not whether it happens under capitalism, communism, or Stalinism."

"Look at what Cuba is doing to help other developing countries," she protested.

"Cuba is, by the way, not a developed country," I cut in. "So there is no chance it can help another underdeveloped country become developed. You cannot give what you do not have. Secondly, Cuba, being itself a country of the South, has very little to lose by helping other poor countries, which would not be the case if the developed countries were to help bring development to the South."

The lesson of the brief encounter related above is that self-interest is no respecter of political ideology. It behaves just the same way, whether under communist or under capitalist influence. In the capitalist system, representatives of private and corporate interests may lead the charge, but those catering to public interests are usually very close by. Under communism, the subdued private interest cedes its role to the state. Despite that distinction in roles, the fact remains that the pursuit of one's own self-interest / corporate or national interests is still paramount and trumps all other considerations. That explains why the defunct Communist Russia was concerned, primarily, with preserving its own interests. That was dictated not by ideology but by the imperatives of self-preservation.

The conclusions I draw and the suggestions that follow thereupon are based on the following premises:

a) That the international setting is constantly changing, so policies similar to those that worked well in the past may prove less successful today in providing a solution to comparable economic problems

b) That the effectiveness of the assistance given by developed countries in promoting or in resisting development in the South increases with the extent to which the developing countries are dependent on the assistance

c) That the existence of developed countries represents both an opportunity for and an obstacle to the development of other countries (which way the scale tips depends greatly on the attitude of the developed countries)

d) That the developed countries will naturally tend to be hostile to all development in the South, which fails to guarantee or which threatens their privileged positions

e) That development in the South, in the long run, threatens rather than guarantees these privileged positions, given the world's limited stock of natural resources and market opportunities

If the premise I put forward here (that the North is in a position to promote or retard development in the South) is accepted, then the need for a new development strategy has been firmly established.

Perhaps the main significance of this short study is to draw the reader's attention to the existence of what may be the greatest of the forces working against development in the South and to warn them of the dangers of ignoring it. I will have achieved the purpose of this book if I succeed in showing that, under present circumstances, there is no reason to believe that economic development, as it is now conceived, will be realized in the South anytime soon. All rhetoric that persuades people in the South to pursue their development objectives along present lines is intended, therefore, to divert their attention from seeking alternative solutions to their problems.

An attempt has been made at reexamining the concept of the international division of labor. In my view, this concept should not be equated with that of international specialization, which demands that countries specialize in the production of those few items for which they enjoy comparative advantages over others. The result of applying such a doctrine is that the poor countries have concentrated on the output of primary products with a very low added-value potential. The concept of the international division of labor should be based on the observation that only those who contribute directly or indirectly in the process of production may lay claims to a part of the output. If you are unemployed, you do not receive any wages. The capitalists or the entrepreneurs who fail to employ their stock will not be rewarded with interests and profits, nor will the property owner who does not succeed in leasing it out receive any rents. The integration of the South in the world economy has resulted in the reduction in the use of the South's resources, with the attendant consequent reduction of their share in the world output of goods and services. It will be reasonable for the South to find a means of increasing their share in the world supply of goods and services by way of an increase in their contribution to the production process. Such an increase can be achieved only if they have a chance to employ profitably their own resources. This calls for some form of protection for the developing economies.

I have had to work with French versions of texts, some of which were originally published in English. All translated quoted texts that appear here are followed by the abbreviation MT, meaning "my translation."

Some effort has been made to ensure accuracy in these translations, and any discrepancies observed therein are, therefore, in no way intentional.

John T. Manga

My own measurement of economic development will be based on such indicators as the availability of the essentials of life, such as drinking water, electricity, food and other such basic commodities in our local markets, at prices within the reach of the lowest income-earner in the country.
—General Buhari, former head of state of Nigeria

Tous les êtres humains aspirent à la santé, à l'éducation, au savoir, à une existence sûre, à un emploi stable, à l'abri des humiliations, à exercer pleinement leur responsabilités politiques et civiles, loin de tout système arbitraire, protégés des malheurs qui offensent leur dignité.
All human beings aspire to good health, to education, to knowledge, to assured existence, to a stable job, to be free from humiliations, to the full exercise of their political and civic responsibilities, away from all arbitrary systems, and protected from any misfortunes that offend their dignity. (MT)
—Jean Ziegler, a Swiss writer

Development means economic, social and political progress. It means a reasonable standard of living, and reasonable in this context requires continual redefinition, what is reasonable in an earlier stage of development will become unreasonable in a later stage,
—Robert S. McNamara, former US defense secretary

CHAPTER I

The Nature Of Development

Defining Development

Those acquainted with the subject matter will probably admit that providing a generally accepted definition of the term *development* is rather difficult. One practice, more or less acceptable, is to spell out the characteristics of a typical developed or underdeveloped country.

In defining underdevelopment, P. Samuelson states,[1]

"An underdeveloped nation is simply one with real per capita income that is low relative to the present-day per-capita incomes of such nations as Canada, the United States, Great Britain and Western Europe generally. Optimistically, an underdeveloped nation is regarded as being capable of substantial increase in its income level."

Some may wish to add to these purely quantitative indicators of an underdeveloped nation other characteristics, such as the following:

- The existence of a very high proportion of the population engaged in agriculture

---

1   P. A. Samuelson, Economics, International Edition (Tokyo: Kohgakusha; McCraw-Hill Books), 741.

- A low level of technology used in industry
- A low level of literacy
- A high rate of child mortality
- A low rate of capital formation
- A low rate of energy consumption, etc.

Ignacy Sachs considers that

"Development must be seen as a societal learning process, the growing ability of a community or a nation; first, to project goals which conform to a set of accepted values— some variant on the theme of equal opportunity for each person to fulfil his or her own potentialities, extended beyond the present to future generation— and then to work towards these goals while keeping within the external constrains inspired by nature and inherited from history."[2]

The Tanzania National Union Party (TANU) believed that

"Development means liberation. Any action that gives the people more control of their own affairs is an action for development . . . Any action that reduces their say in determining their own affairs or running their own lives is not development and retards them . . . , it is of first importance to place a lot of emphasis on improving (the people's) conditions . . ."[3]

A major setback in the definitions of the term *development* as advanced by many economists is that they tend to use the same criteria that serve to measure economic growth. Although one may engender the other, there

---

2 Ignacy Sachs, "Crises of Maldevelopment in the North: A Way Out" (International Forum for Development Alternatives [IFDA], Dossier N°2, Nov. 1978), 4.

3 Reginald Green, "The Basic Human Needs: A Strategic Conceptualization toward Another Development" (International Forum for Development Alternatives [IFDA], Dossier N°2, Nov. 1978), 3.

is a great difference between the two concepts. Stated briefly, economic growth involves increases in output, whereas economic development is concerned, first, with structural change. This distinction shows the extent to which present-day yardsticks for measuring development are inadequate. Defining development in terms of per capita income level leaves much to be desired, especially where income is expressed in nominal rather than in real terms. Moreover, there is no agreed level below which per capita income is considered to be low. This means that revenue level is high or low relative to other known levels. Such a criterion is best suited to the measurement of changes in income levels of a given society. In other words, it is best suited to the measurement of economic growth. Economic development is a less palpable phenomenon, with hardly any objective means by which to measure it. While development implies structural changes involving more or less the entire society, economic growth can take place in isolated sectors of the economy. The income level of a nation, as measured by its gross national product (GNP), may actually rise without there being any substantial improvement in the overall standard of living.

In view of the above difficulty, instead of stating what development means, I will rather try to answer the following questions: What is the purpose of economic development? In other words, why does society need to develop? What do we expect to achieve through development?

The purpose of development, it seems, is to bring satisfaction to the needs of society. I hasten to add here that these needs are in no way limited to the most basic ones. Development must be seen as a process by which society seeks to (to borrow Jeremy Bentham's expression) increase pleasures (or well-being) and to decrease pain (or displeasures). Development is promoted primarily by the desire to lighten the burdens that nature has placed on life: the need to eat, the need to drink, the need to rest, the need to maintain one's body temperature within a certain range, the need to stay healthy, the need for communication, the need for protection from danger, the need to work, the need to feel strong and to maintain one's dignity, etc. Development involves the acquisition and use of knowledge and skills by society through learning, trial and error, practice, and mimicking. It is a process—the learning process—that enables the incremental buildup of capacities, which, in turn, result in structural change. It comes complete with its own culture. Development is important for its ability to provide a country with increased capacities (productive, absorptive, and consumptive). All three of these are important if a country needs to develop further.

Francis Hackett spells out what he expects of development in the following words:

> *"I believe in materialism. I believe in all proceeds of a healthy materialism,—good cooking, dry houses, dry feet, sewers, drain pipes, hot water, baths, electric lights, automobiles, good roads, bright streets, long vacations away from the village pump, new ideas, fast horses, swift conversations, theatres, operas, orchestras, bands. I believe in them all for everybody. The man who dies without knowing these things may be as exquisite as a saint, and as rich as a poet; but it is in spite of, not because of his deprivation."*[4]

There is obviously a link between satisfying the needs of society and the production of goods and services. Needs—be they those of society as a whole or those of individuals within it—can be met only if there exist the means of satisfying them. The need to travel can be satisfied only if there are sufficient means of travel—at reasonable costs. Therefore, in seeking satisfaction for our needs, we have to produce, create, or acquire objects or services we think are capable of achieving these aims. These objects or services are not in themselves the purposes of development. They are only the means to achieving that objective, which we have stated as the satisfaction of our needs.

---

4   Francis Hackett, Ireland, quoted by P. A. Samuelson in Economics (see above), chap. 39.

Since the satisfaction of needs calls for the existence of goods and services (which are often scarce), the task of development, therefore, consists of producing those goods and services it takes to satisfy these needs. Knowing that needs are constantly changing and increasing, development aims at finding ways of satisfying them on permanent or long-term bases. The provision of a cup of water to a thirsty person may satisfy this immediate need but does nothing to satisfy his or her long-term need for drinking water. As the law of diminishing returns comes into play, the tendency is to introduce other, more efficient methods that are capable of holding back the invading constraints, be they natural or man-made. The task of development can, therefore, be conceived as involving a continuous search for means of providing for society's needs, both immediate and future.

The choice of a development model depends (should I say, ought to depend) on the accepted priorities of society. It goes without saying that there is no standard scale of values for all societies. In a country where temperatures are relatively low, the need to incorporate air conditioners into buildings is less urgent than in another where temperatures are high. Whatever the natural setting or conditions of a country, common sense demands that the so-called basic needs be satisfied first. Not only are development priorities different for different nations, but the means of achieving them can also differ. Two countries with apparently identical problems may choose to solve them in quite different ways, the choice of a solution being dependent on the available resources as well as their respective values and assumptions.

Development is intended to serve the interests of the entire society. Francis Hackett, in the text quoted above, expressed this concern for the interest of society when he said, ". . . I believe in them all for everybody." "Any action that gives the people more control of their own affairs is an action for development," so said the TANU. Adam Smith justified his case for liberalism in political economy by arguing that it was the best way to serve the general interest of society. The purpose of development would, therefore, be defeated if it failed to address itself to problems of general interests to society.

In stating the purpose of development, it was suggested that it is a problem-solving process. Anything that does not seek to provide a solution to human problems is, therefore, not contributing to development. And anything that has the net effect of increasing rather than reducing these problems may be said to be contributing to maldevelopment.

Up to a certain point in history, it was felt that there could be no harm in employing methods aimed at reducing labor inputs in production. Indeed, it was considered humanitarian—although entrepreneurs had quite other reasons for seeking to reduce labor demands—to strive to reduce what was then seen as a burden on workers. Things have since changed; so that any further measures taken to cut down the demand for labor, at least in certain areas of economic activity, are increasingly being seen as creating more problems than they seek to solve. So when labor-cutting methods start making labor redundant, thus creating unemployment, we must see them as working against the objectives of development as just stated above.

The need for every normal, able-bodied person to work can hardly be overemphasized. Voltaire's title character, Candide, after several months of travels and troubles, came to the simple conclusion that it was *'wise to cultivate one's own garden. For that kept one away from three great ills; boredom, vice and want.'*[5]

The great English poet William Cowper was to state his case for work in the following lines:

> *"Absence of occupation is not rest,*
> *A mind quite vacant is a mind distressed."*

According to the objectives of development just stated above, distress, boredom, and want—facets of Bentham's pain or displeasure—all need

---

5   Voltaire, Candide, ou l'Optimisme (Paris: Hachette, Nouveaux classiques illustrés, 1976), 177.

to be decreased, not increased. Given that they all occur as a result of lack of work or occupation, it follows that the provision of opportunity for work is, or should be, an objective of development.

Contrary to what some scriptures suggest, work is not a curse; it is, perhaps, an integral part of the true paradise of man. And talking about scriptures, the Baha'i faith talks of the *'exaltation of work, performed in the spirit of service, to the rank of worship.'*[6]

According to E. F. Schumacher, *"Buddhism takes the function of work to be at least threefold: to give man a chance to utilize and develop his faculties; to enable him to overcome his ego-centeredness by joining with other people in a common task; and to bring forth the goods and services needed for a becoming existence."*[7]

The economist John M. Keynes addresses some of the problems that the absence of occupation (or unemployment) might bring when he writes,

". . . if the economic problem is solved, mankind will be deprived of its traditional purpose.

Will this be a benefit? If one believes at all in the real values of life, the prospect at least opens up the possibility of benefit. Yet I think with dread of the readjustment of the habits and the instincts of the ordinary man, bred into him for countless generations, which he may be asked to discard within a few decades.

To use the language of today—must we not expect a general "nervous breakdown of a kind which is already common enough in England and the United States among the wives of the well-to-do classes, unfortunate women, many of them, who have been deprived of their traditional tasks and occupations—who cannot find it sufficiently amusing, when deprived of the spur of economic necessity, to cook

---

6   Shoghi Effendi, God Passes By, 19.7, 281.

7   E. F. Schumacher, Small Is Beautiful: A Study of Economics as if People Mattered (New York: Harper and Row, Publishers, 1973), 54-55.

and clean and mend, yet are quite unable to find anything more amusing. "[8]

The economic problems of nations (even the most developed ones amongst them) are still very far from completely solved. But already, symptoms of Keynes's "general nervous breakdown" are beginning to appear, especially among the jobless. And theirs is a yet more serious problem than those of the wives of the well-to-do classes. Unlike these housewives who may be exposed only to boredom, the absence of occupation exposes the jobless to both boredom and want. Without actually providing a solution to the problems of human needs, certain kinds of technology may, indeed, accentuate some of these very problems as well as create other ones. Technological development has not always reckoned with the need for man to have some form of occupation at all times.

The psychologist B. F. Skinner, in the introduction to his well-known novel *Walden Two*, wrote,

> *"The basic research has also shown how important it is for everyone, young and old, women and men, not only to receive goods but to engage in their production. (. . .)*
>
> *There are many ways of saving labor, but they should not, (. . .) be used to save laborers and hence to increase unemployment."*[9]

Just as work was once a burden to man, the absence of work has increasingly become a burden too. Unemployment, as has just been argued above, is a problem today insofar as it exposes us to pain or displeasure. In just a short time, thinking and behavior have evolved from the biblical concept of work as punishment to work as a fulfilment, a need. It has become a problem born of the decoupling of the dual

8   John M. Keynes, Essays in Persuasion: Economic Possibilities for Our Grandchildren (England: St. Martin's Press, for the Royal Economic Society, 1972), 327.

9   See B. F. Skinner, *Walden Two* [New York: Macmillan Publishers, 1976], X.

functions of work, which are its role as a factor of production and its role in satisfying a physiological human need. The employer is primarily interested in work only as an economic input. But it is an input that the same employer is doing everything possible to replace with machines. In doing so, the employer is merely responding to the demands of self-interest, which are usually behind most decisions he or she makes. The growing scarcity of opportunities for work needs to be added to the list of problems that the development process must address. Work must be seen as having a physiological function—which needs to be fulfilled—in addition to its function as a factor of production. People work not only for the money or wealth that working brings them but also for a wide range of other reasons, including the satisfaction they derive from working. If money or material reward were the only motives for working, then some of the richest people in the world like Warren Buffett and Bill Gates would not have any more reasons to work. It is very well-known that an important challenge to society today is its ability to provide each and every one of its members with the opportunity to work as long and as much as they need to. Governments have been voted into office with the hope, if not on the promise, that they would create or facilitate the creating of jobs for their populations. Other governments have been voted out of office or brought down by some other means because they failed to adequately meet their people's need for work. Since the crisis of the first half of last century, the functions of the state have expanded to include the strife for what has come to be called full employment. The need to facilitate the creation of jobs has become such an important issue in politics that no government (not even those of market economies that are not directly involved in job creation) can afford to ignore the expectation of its voters with regard to job availability. So not just the right to work but also the probability of finding work has become a legitimate demand of the people on society.

Work, of one kind or the other, is a necessary function of human life not only for the opportunity it offers to satisfy our material needs but also for its own sake.

John M. Keynes stresses this point when he says,

". . . For many ages to come the old Adam will be strong in us that everybody will need to do some work if he has to be contented. We shall do more things for ourselves to be contented. We shall do more things for ourselves than is usual with the rich today, only too glad to have small duties and tasks and routines. But beyond this, we shall endeavour to spread the bread thin over the butter—to make what work there is still to be done to be as widely spread as possible."[10]

Abraham Maslow's hierarchy of needs does not specifically mention work as a human need. It is, however, obvious that man needs to work in order to satisfy most of the needs he enumerated therein. Viewed in that context, work can be seen as a physiological need that must be satisfied. Unfortunately, as society becomes more developed, the chances of meeting this growing demand for jobs become harder and harder. Gone are the days when industry was short of labor and children as young as twelve years old were compelled to work as many as seventy hours a week. Today, not even adults can find work easily. So where has all the work gone?

At least, a partial answer to this question can be traced back to the constant pursuit of what economists call productivity, which the *Britannica Concise Encyclopedia* defines as "a measure of productive efficiency calculated as the ratio of what is produced to what is required to produce it." There is said to be labor productivity gains when the output per unit of labor increases or, in what amounts to the same thing, when the same amount of output is obtained by applying a smaller amount of labor.

---

10   Keynes, Essays in Persuasion, 327.

Productivity gains are achieved primarily through technological innovation and improvements in management or production processes. Productivity gains can contribute to improved living standards in that when they occur, more value is added to production, which results in greater income being earned or distributed. The problem remains of how the increased income is distributed. That is, how much of the gains does labor receive? It is the same old problem that Adam Smith identified a long time ago and whose examination led him to the conclusion that

> *"It is not, however, difficult to foresee which of the two parties must, upon all ordinary occasions, have the advantage in the dispute, and force the other into a compliance with their terms. (. . .) But though in disputes with their workmen, masters must generally have the advantage, . . ."*[11]

Gains in productivity have their downside, too. Where they lead to the production of goods and services over and above what the market can absorb, they may lead to the reduction in the quantities of input required to produce what is needed to satisfy demand. Labor is usually amongst the first input categories to be curtailed. Therefore, improvements in productivity may engender labor redundancy, which may, in turn, lead to Bentham's pain or displeasure.

Ever since employers and employees have been fighting over the sharing of the proceeds of production, the employers have been working hard to reduce the importance of labor as an input, hence their potential to create pain.

Indeed, the introduction of machines into industry has gone a long way to lighten the burdens placed on the workers. Technological innovation has given rise to new industries and has transformed old ones, too. It has also created new jobs and enabled the production of a vast variety of products that did not exist before. It has also lowered

---

11   Adam Smith, *The Wealth of Nations* (New York: Bantam Books, 2003), 94-96.

the cost of producing a great number of items. Unfortunately, the rate at which technological innovation has enabled the creation of new jobs has been too slow to compensate for the ones suppressed. The overall effect of innovation has been a rise in output per worker, which has gradually rendered some workers redundant—for lack of demand. In the case of technology introduced from abroad, no real compensation may be expected for the lost jobs.

Development, as it is currently represented, is a problem-solving as well as a problem-generating process. For a long time, the use of labor in production was considered an inconvenience that needed to be reduced to the minimum possible. As we have just seen, the increasing replacement of labor-intensive processes with capital-intensive ones has displaced labor and rendered it increasingly redundant. So the quest for near-labor-free production (a questionable development objective, by the way) has engendered the present, undesirable condition of job scarcity—a new problem that the development process must now strive to resolve. As living conditions improve (another development objective), the tendency would be for the population to grow. And with that growth come problems associated with large populations. Again, by seeking to lighten the burdens of human existence, development is creating other problems, which it will have to address sooner or later. Development is, therefore, a problem-creating process too.

Pollution results primarily from the process of transforming materials and consuming goods and services. Most natural resources cannot be consumed in their original state. They have to undergo some form of transformation. In the process, however, production waste occurs, which, unless properly handled, will go on to create other environmental problems. And the solving of those problems will, in turn, become a development objective.

Even if population were constant and pollution checked, because of the insatiability of human beings, there would still be demand for all that is considered valuable. People easily get tired of consuming a given product and ask for other improved ones. Motorists always want new vehicles that run faster or that offer greater comfort or more security or a combination of some of these qualities. The housewives ask for more sophisticated household equipment. Doctors dream of ever more effective ways of combating disease. So all this places continuous demand on development.

Development is also an endless process. It may be pursued for reasons that vary greatly with both time and place. In underdeveloped societies, where even the most basic needs still go unattended for the overwhelming majority of the people, the driving force behind the development process is (or ought to be) the desire to meet these basic needs. This would not be the case in the developed societies where there are abundant supplies of those goods required to satisfy basic needs. In the latter societies, the urge for continued development stems from the desire to attain or to maintain society's position—the need to avoid lagging behind or being surpassed by other societies. Growth and technical innovation become development goals in their own right. There is a feeling of paranoid fear behind the urge for growth and technological innovation. There is a constant fear of losing one's privileged position, the fear of being surpassed by some newcomer or rival. Profit making too becomes a major goal as development takes on the character of athletic competition. It is the prestige and the standing of the developed societies that are at stake here. And as John K. Galbraith suggests, it is only by technical innovation that the developed societies can expect to hold their ground against newcomers.[12] Technical advancement, on which their capacity for expansion is dependent, is thus enshrined as a social good.

If research on the development of labor-saving machines is allowed to continue unchecked, it will become possible to eliminate human labor entirely. And if that were to happen, where would it leave mankind? Such a prospect is compatible only with socialism. For it is

---

12   John K. Galbraith, excerpt from "The New Industrial State," Business Strategy, ed. H. Igor Ansoff (repr., Penguin Modern Management Reading, 1977), 213-214.

only in socialist societies that all citizens have a right to a share of the economy's output—the means of production being a collective property. In a market economy, only the owners of those factors of production which actually entered into production would be rightfully entitled to a share of the output. A squeeze on employment arising from technical innovation will, therefore, marginalize an increasing number of people. If the squeeze on employment opportunities in developed countries is not as pronounced as it ought to be today, it is because this adverse effect of technical innovation is partially cushioned off by exports to the Third World. If Third World markets for European industrial goods did not exist, it would mean that nearly 40 percent of European export goods would not find a market. So, many of those Europeans who owe their jobs to the export market would be without employment. In other words, markets in the South compensate greatly for jobs lost in the North as a result of technical innovation.

Even if the level of development were the same for all countries, the prospects of diminishing job opportunities might not be a strong enough deterrent against labor-saving technical innovation. For self-interest concerns will always dictate what decisions investors take. If such an innovation (harmful as it may be to society but not prohibited by law) offered a chance for the investors to improve their earnings or reduce their losses, they surely would not hesitate to undertake it. Their decision is, indeed, a part of their struggle to keep up not only with the growing productive tasks created by ecological pressures but also with competition within their own society. In the market economies, where such competitive pressures are greatest and where the adverse effects of labor-saving technology are likely to be most evident, it will be a great surprise if individual decision makers were to agree to a kind of "technological truce." Although there may be a consensus for the control of the pace of technical progress in order to prevent it from running amok, the priority that each individual decider gives to his or her own interests impels them to take decisions that militate against such a consensus, hence the technical advancement (which sometimes runs) in the wrong direction.

Explaining Development

Let us now turn to the question of how the countries of the North became more developed than those of the South. The Industrial Revolution in England will be of particular interest here, for it was the first and, perhaps, the best known of industrial revolutions. The accelerated development that took place in England can be seen as linked with the process of industrialization in that country. Explaining development there would invariably mean explaining the process of industrialization.

At the time of the Industrial Revolution, England witnessed a period of sustained growth. Both the home and agricultural markets were expanding rapidly. England's commercial undertakings around the world opened up huge markets for both finished goods and raw materials. The means of transportation (canals, good roads, and later, railroads) were cheap and easy, which made it possible to transport goods relatively quickly across the country. Her geographical position was favorable to the development of the shipping industry. At the time, it could be said that England possessed the technical know-how necessary for an economic takeoff. She did not have to depend on imported technology. Moreover, the technical requirements of the time were fairly simple. All that was required was a sufficiency of people with ordinary familiarity with simple mechanical devices and the working of metal, practical experience, and initiative.

Linked with the problem of technical know-how was that of capital. Most industrial undertakings at the time did not involve huge capital layouts. There was an abundant supply of labor. Small farmers who lost their lands were available for employment in the factories. The gradual abolition of enclosures forced farmers to turn to the factories for jobs. Labor was, therefore, abundant and, what was more, cheap.

War seemed to have played an important role in the industrial expansion of England. As in most other developed countries, wars were important for at least two reasons: they encouraged the development and the use of modern technology, and they opened up new markets for English manufactures.

According to E. J. Hobsbawm,

"The country which succeeded in concentrating other people's export markets, or even in monopolizing the export markets of a large part of the world in a sufficiently brief period of time, could expand its export industries at a rate sometimes virtually compulsory. And that was what Britain succeeded in doing in the eighteenth century."[13]

Such success could not have been achieved without the use of force, hence the development of modern technologies in warfare, which were later adapted to the civilian economy. Those sectors of the economy concerned with the production of military hardware were encouraged, if not obliged, to expand. The magnitude of demand was such that manufacturers had difficulties keeping pace with it. Unlike today, England could not at the time expect to receive military supplies from abroad, so only the home economy was relied upon to supply the armies.

Above all things, England had a powerful government that was ready to come to the rescue of the economy in times of need. It was a government that had the courage and the power to destroy competition in foreign markets in order to create favorable business conditions for her citizens.[14] Despite the growing importance of the manufacturing sector, commerce still accounted for a very great part of the wealth the economy produced. England owed a lot to her trade, especially her trade with the underdeveloped world.

---

13   E. J. Hobsbawm, "Industry and Empire," The Pelican Economic History of Britain, vol. 3 (repr., England: Penguin Books, 1980), 39.

14   Ibid.

These special circumstances no longer exist today. Governments of developing countries are not powerful enough to have any real impact on the international scene (some of them are not even in control of their home situation). Wars cannot be expected to provide incentives for the local development of technology, for most of the military equipment they need today are supplied by the developed countries. If wars in the Southern countries achieve anything, it is to provide the opportunity to test weapons conceived and produced in the advanced countries. Economic spin-offs from such military experiments accrue not to the belligerent countries of the South but to their suppliers in the North. This only serves to aggravate the already weak economic standing of developing countries.

Theories Of The Stages Of Growth

Some of the economists who have studied the nature of economic development have come up with what may be termed theories of economic development.

Adam Smith argued that there were four distinct stages in the evolution of society. Each of them was characterized by the chief occupation of the time. They were, in order of chronology, hunting, animal breeding, agriculture, and commerce and industry. This does not in any way mean that, at any given time, there was practiced only one of the four occupations. Two or even three of them must have been practiced simultaneously. What is important here is that each stage was characterized by one dominant activity. Smith's thesis (at least, in what concerns the first three stages) suggests that evolution from one phase to another was not motivated by the desire to attain some far-removed, predetermined goal, such as mass consumption. It came as a means of adapting society to the evolving environmental situation. As time went by, the readily available stock of wild animals decreased, with the result that hunting became less and less rewarding. The rearing of animals seemed a means of ensuring the steady supply of meat for consumption.

Thus, society evolved from one stage to another. It is difficult to say when each of the various stages started in any given society.

German authors of the late nineteenth century thought that nations evolved from slavery to pastoral activities, then to agricultural, and finally, to industry and commerce.

Karl Marx thought that the various stages of growth were characterized by the existence or the absence of the right to private ownership of property. In the first stage, there was no private property. That was the period he called primitive communism. Then came stage two, characterized by the private ownership of slaves. Stage three was reached with the private ownership of land. Marx called this the period of feudalism. The fourth stage, that of capitalism, was reached when the private ownership of the means of production became generalized. By introducing the concept of private ownership in his analysis of the various stages of social evolution, Marx gave a hint on why society (at least, the influential part of it) became interested in the fostering of economic growth. People were urged on by their desire to augment their stock of private property, to protect their individual interests, and to maintain or to improve their privileged positions in society. Marx foresaw two other stages: socialism and, finally, communism. In Marx's own view, growth came not out of the desire to adapt society to the shifting ecological setting but out of the desire of individuals to better their lot. The decision to improve the means of production was, therefore, made on individual basis and not as a result of a consensus on the part of society.

In *The Stages of Economic Growth*, W. W. Rostow spells out five stages of development through which all nations have to pass. These are the traditional society, the preconditions for a takeoff, the takeoff, the drive to maturity, and the age of mass consumption. According to this author, the stage of traditional society is one where society is still in its pre-Newtonian stage, i.e., where the use of scientific and technical knowledge in the production process is nonexistent. The second stage, that of the preconditions for a takeoff, is characterized by the incorporation, for the first time, of scientific and technical knowledge into production processes. During this period, society prepares itself for the full exploitation of the fruits of modern science. Next comes the takeoff period when final resistance to modernization is broken and the old methods of production are entirely replaced. As production increases beyond the subsistence level, capital accumulation (with the accompanying compound interests) becomes possible. Maturity, which is the fourth stage, is reached some sixty years after the takeoff. Rostow defines it as the stage *"in which an economy demonstrates the capacity to move beyond the original industries which powered its take-off and to high efficiency over a very wide range of its resources."*[15]

The age of high mass consumption is the final stage of this scenario. It is reached when the leading sectors shift toward durable consumer goods and services, a phase from which "Americans are beginning to emerge." According to Rostow, what stands out clear from the foregoing thesis is that development, be it economic or social, is a continuing process of change. The rate of change is generally irregular, high at one time and low at another. This change (let us call it aggregate change) is the sum of a great number of other smaller changes taking place in society. Some of these smaller changes are only indirectly (if at all) related to one another. Although development implies change, not all change is development. There is a change for the better just as there is a change for the worse. We shall understand here that only a change for the better contributes to development.

The partitioning of the process of economic development into stages is left to the judgment of each author. The criteria are altogether arbitrary; so too is the number of stages he or she chooses to establish. Adam Smith and Turgot thought there were only four stages. Marx thought there were six. Rostow identified five stages, ranging from the primitive society to that of high mass consumption. Adam Smith's stages were characterized by the chief occupation of the time. Those of Karl

---

15   W. W. Rostow, The Stages of Growth (Cambridge, 1960), 9-10.

Marx bore the features of the mode of production and the social rapport based on property rights. Rostow came up with a completely new set of criteria based on the level of economic capacity of a society and its ability to incorporate modern technology into its production processes and to accumulate capital necessary for further investments.

Not even the authorities of a country with a centrally planned economic system can claim to control all the factors affecting development. Attempting to plan economic development with a view to achieving some predetermined long-term goals seems a bit unrealistic. All that the central authority can do is to provide the right atmosphere and the structure on which development can build. The government can provide the needed social overhead capital (good communication networks and the appropriate education) and the guarantees that come with the rule of law. It can directly invest in certain sectors of the economy or encourage such investments by others. All that, even though essential, is not sufficient to ensure economic development.

A very common way of enriching one-self at the expense of others is through commerce.

—Botero, an Italian writer

Certes, nous encourageons l'aide qui nous aide à nous passer de l'aide.

(Indeed, we welcome aid that helps us forgo aid.)

—Capt. Thomas Sankara, late president of Burkina Faso

We have always known that heedless self-interest was bad morals; we know now that it is bad economics.

—FDR (in second inaugural speech)

CHAPTER II

Some Factors Affecting Development

Choice Of Development Model

The planning of economic development involves a lot of decision making. Not only does it require choosing and arranging objectives according to a given scale of values, but it also involves decisions concerning the means of attaining the chosen objectives. In many developing countries, the narrowing of the gap between them and the developed countries is considered a major objective of development. This has invariably meant imitating the developed countries and accepting, without questioning, development models conceived for their own societies. It is clear, however, that development cannot mean the same thing to both groups of societies. And even if it did, the means of attaining determined goals would not necessarily be the same. As was suggested in the previous section, the driving force behind development or technical progress is both time and space variant.

Making the wrong choice of priorities and of the means of attaining them can, indeed, constitute a whole lot of obstacles. In trying to imitate the North, developing countries fail to recognize the vast difference between their development priorities and those of developed countries. This has often led them to adopt policies similar to those that succeeded in the North, irrespective of the fact that the social and economic contexts of both groups of societies are not in any way similar. Economic doctrine that calls for development through foreign trade was successful in bringing about change in the now-developed countries. Whether it is capable of producing similar results today is yet to be shown.

The question of choice has not seemed a major issue to development planners in the South. The reason for this is that they are given to believe that there already exist models that they can adopt. At face value, that is, indeed, a very attractive offer that only very few developing countries can think of rejecting. But a major danger in imitating the North (a danger still ignored by many) is that the developing countries make the success of their efforts to develop dependent on the attitude of the North, thus increasing the latter's leverage effect on them. This means that development in the South can be postponed or even prevented if it is judged likely to produce negative effects in the North.

Capital Formation And Acquisition Of Resource Mix

For the purpose of this work, we shall adopt Irving Fisher's concept of capital, which is defined as "any asset which yields a stream of income over time." In this sense, the term no longer refers exclusively to physical goods but also to all other forms of resources accumulated and set aside for the production of goods and services. Money, machines, raw materials, land, technology, and finished goods are only some of the forms that capital can take.

For most societies, a large part of capital formation still results from savings, i.e., abstinence from the immediate consumption of resources for the purpose of reinvesting them.

A classical explanation of the perpetual problem of capital shortage in the poor countries runs thus: The people are poor. So they cannot save. Since they cannot save, they cannot raise capital, and consequently, they cannot invest. And since they cannot invest, they cannot improve their productive capacities. And since these capacities cannot be improved upon, they cannot raise their income level. And since they cannot raise their income level, they cannot save.

It would be grossly misleading to imagine that capital formation is impossible in most Third World countries. The existence of mass poverty in these countries does not mean that there are no rich people in there.

It is well-known that the ability of individuals to save decreases with their income level. The less they earn, the less they can afford to set aside as savings. But as the revenue of wage earners or of land owners decreases, that of the other categories of income earners may, indeed, be increasing. For a fixed output level, the volume of savings is determined by both the propensity to save and the structure of income distribution. The pattern of income distribution in many Third World countries is such that savings or capital formation ought to be easy to achieve. There is a concentration of wealth in the hands of the few. [16]

This ought to allow for easy capital formation and investment. The low level of income of the masses is, therefore, not a major obstacle to capital formation. Not every individual needs to save for there to be capital formation capabilities in a country.

However, only a relatively small proportion of people in the poor countries are wage earners. In some cases, as much as 70 percent of the active population are self-employed people. As with all other groups of income earners, their ability to save depends largely on their income level and their propensity to save. But their income level is determined by both their output level and the exchange rate for their products. Where the exchange rate is favorable and output substantial, their level of income will be high, and their ability to save should be high too. Presently, the rate of exchange for farm produce from Third World

---

16   In Gabon, the average per capita income for the richest 20 percent of the population was thirty-five times as much as that of the poorest 20 percent. In Colombia, the ratio was thirty-one to one, whereas in Brazil, it was seventeen to one. (See Adelman and Morris in An Anatomy of Income Distribution Patterns in Developing Nations, IBRD mimeo. WP 116, September 1971.)

countries is generally unfavorable. This explains, at least partially, their low income level as well as their inability to save. A good part of the fruits of their labor accrues to the numerous middlemen who make up the supply chain stretching up to the final consumer.

The capacity for capital formation in the Third World is further reduced by its very high propensity to consume. Not all consumption militates against capital formation. What really happens is that the process of capital formation is extended several steps further. If the rich in the poor countries spend their wealth on luxury goods and if their governments too invest in prestige projects, occasions may be created for capital accumulation by the local entrepreneur class. If such ostentatious goods and services are imported rather than produced locally, the local economy will not benefit from it. But if it calls for massive use of local resources (labor, raw materials, and technology), the capacity for capital accumulation will be greatly enhanced. The income of the suppliers of these local resources will rise. As a good part of the earnings of a great majority of the local suppliers of resources will not necessarily be spent on imported luxury goods, an occasion may be provided for savings to go up. This group of income earners will also stimulate the economy by consuming local products.

The debt burden constitutes a very great obstacle to capital accumulation. One reason for the growing burden is the unfavorable terms under which much of the debts are contracted. For instance, certain loans are granted on condition that the borrowing country accepts to purchase from the one granting the loan. The cost to the borrower-country of such goods and services is generally well above what obtains on the open market.

Capital formation in the Third World is also made difficult by the net outflow of resources. Transfer pricing, overpricing, and direct expatriation are only a few of the methods used to transfer funds out of the poor countries. Between 1960 and 1966, United States private investments in Latin America amounted to 2.7 billion dollars while revenue from these investments transferred home amounted to 8.3 billion dollars. In 1972 alone, Switzerland extracted 465 million francs from the LDCs whereas its investments there amounted to only 344 million francs.[17]

A country's expenditure on education and health, for instance, is to be considered as capital expenditure, just in the same way as would be expenditure on machinery. The value of labor supply resulting from such expenditure forms an integral part of the country's stock of social overhead capital just as do the health and educational institutions that produce the labor. These investments on labor development are as important to the economy as are investments on producer goods.

In a short article titled "Rising Expectations Must be Postponed," Calvin B. Hoover, talking about capital formation, suggested that the unwillingness of leaders of some developing countries to repeat the experience of the West 'was a reflection of repudiation in most underdeveloped countries of the economic system of capitalism under which industrialization took place in the advanced countries.'[18] What was this economic system that the leaders of these nascent countries were thus repudiating? Again, a look at the history of the Industrial Revolution in England allows us a glimpse of how at least part of capital formation was achieved there. We read from Eric Williams's book, *Capitalism and Slavery* that slavery and slave trade contributed substantially to capital formation in England. The wealth accumulated from the triangular trade, of which slave trade and slavery were no small part, contributed to the financing of the Industrial Revolution. He writes,

"The sundry assortment was typical of the slave trader's cargo. Finery for Africans, household utensils, cloths of all kinds, iron and other metals, together with guns, handcuffs and fetters: the production of these stimulated capitalism, provided employment for British labour, and brought great profits to England".[19]

17   Rudolf H. Strahn, Pays Industrialisés, Pays Sous-développés: Faits et Chiffres (Bern: A la Baconnière, 1974), 102 and 116.

18   *Readings in Economics*, 4th ed. (1964), 357.

19   Eric Williams, *Capitalism and Slavery*, 65.

Some of the very people who had taken part in the triangular trade later converted to other more *respectable* businesses. The transition often went from tradesman to merchant and then to banker or to industrialist. Money earned from trading activities with both West Africa and the West Indies was thus invested in banking, in heavy industries, in insurance companies, etc. Adam Smith was opposed to only one aspect of the trade: monopoly. To him, it represented nothing but the sacrifice of the general good to the interests of a few, the sacrifice of the interest of the home consumer to that of the colonial producer.

Monopoly might have been detrimental to the general good, but it certainly was conducive to the formation of capital since it enabled the owners of monopolies to accumulate wealth as quickly as possible. If the interests of the colonial producer (the monopolists) had been sacrificed in favor of the home consumer, capital formation would have been made much more difficult. The general good is said to be served where there is no monopoly precisely because the price of goods and services tends to fall as producers compete for market shares. Not so with a monopolistic market, which offers greater prospects for capital accumulation—to the detriment of the consumer.

For production to take place, there need to be at hand the resources (human and material) required by the chosen production method. Given the uneven distribution of resources over the globe, only few countries are endowed with all the resources they need to produce most of the goods and services they consume. A general practice is to import those resources that cannot be obtained locally—at a reasonable cost—and to export those that are not needed for domestic use.

Obtaining an optimal resource mix is crucial to the efficient use of productive factors. By optimal resource mix, I mean the different elements needed to produce (most efficiently) a given good or service, for instance, technology, raw materials, finished or semifinished products, specialized labor, fuel, etc. Difficulties encountered by developing countries in obtaining an optimal resource mix are rooted in the cost of those resources they need to import from other countries. The process of importing such resources is often bedeviled by the following:

- The reluctance with which owners of certain resources (technology, for instance) agree to transfer them
- The limited absorptive capacity of certain countries (the smallest unit of equipment that a manufacturer may be willing to supply may be too large for the market that the importer intends to service)
- The high cost that certain importing countries are made to pay for such resources, etc.

This is especially the case with the transfer of technology and technical expertise. A lot of resistance can be observed on the part of industrialized countries to the transfer of technical resources. For instance, the ASEAN countries have been complaining of Japan's unwillingness to reveal its high-tech know-how. The attitude of Japan, as well as that of most developed countries, is reflected in this remark of a Japanese diplomat to his Malaysian critic: *"There is a quid pro quo involved in these transactions. What has Malaysia to offer?"*

The diplomat's remark does not in any way imply that developing countries are unwilling to pay for the technology they seek to acquire. The truth of the matter is that in the face of potential threat from developing nations, owners of technology are no longer satisfied with pecuniary compensation. Japan itself is a living example of those countries who owe their economic success to the transfer of technology. Today, Japan is stronger than most of those countries from whom it imported technology. The fear is that history could repeat itself and that those who receive Japanese technology today would become their rivals tomorrow.

Technology

Technology for industry is either developed locally or imported. Much of the technology now used in production in the Third World was transferred from the North.

However, the transfer has not been without much burden to developing countries. Developing nations are known to import industrial equipment and other goods at highly inflated prices. Of the five million dollars in pharmaceutical imports into Colombia in 1974, three million (i.e., 60 percent) were payments in excess of world prices.[20] The Ivory Coast paid between 10 percent and 40 percent above market price for each of the five sugar refineries it bought from France in the mid-seventies.[21]

Added to the depleting effects of the transfer process are those inherent in oversized industries. Factories operating at well below full capacity abound in many Third World countries. Commenting on the sale of excessively large factory equipment to certain African countries, the French weekly, *L'Expansion* states,

> *". . . Africa has served as a hunting ground to amateur industrialists . . . Mills condemned in advance to operate at a loss . . . Many of which have become ghost factories, sumptuous and gigantic constructions . . . For example, the textile mills sold to Bangui or to Bamako or Niamey by the Willot group of companies; or the one sold to Togo by Voye; the University complex in Madagascar built by Jean-Baptiste Doumeng . . .*
>
> *Indeed, the French are not the only ones to get swept into this opening. But the remarks of an expatriate executive (. . .) are, unfortunately, typical of a certain mentality: 'We are here to make money, not to suck Nivaquine'."[22] (MT)*

Sudan's railway corporation wanted to replace its faulty semiautomatic signals with new ones. But the manufacturers were unable to honor the order because the production of semiautomatic signals had been

---

20   *Jeune Afrique Economie*, no. 38 (Paris, April 1984), 62-3.

21   *L'Expansion* (Paris, Oct. 21-Nov. 3, 1983), 183.

22   *GEO* (Paris, Dec. 1983), 20.

discontinued some ten years earlier. A representative of the manufacturers advised the railway authorities to order an entirely automatic system. He added, ". . . *we will supply it as soon as possible.*"[23] Some of the costly equipment imported by developing countries have had to be abandoned in this manner just because their producers have stopped making spare parts or stopped servicing them. Thus the importers of such equipment are forced to buy new ones each time their suppliers in the industrialized countries decide to renew their products. The rate of change is so fast that imported capital goods become obsolete long before they have been fully amortized. Competition is so keen in the industrialized countries that some equipment become obsolete very quickly, with the result that manufacturers stop producing their spare parts even though there may still be a market for them in the developing countries.

The high cost of technology may also be attributed to the restrictive clauses in the transfer contracts under which the licensee firms undertake not to export goods produced with the help of the transferred technology to certain countries. This is, indeed, a great handicap, for the market area in which the firms are allowed to operate may be too small for them to use the acquired equipment profitably.

The transfer of technology makes the country or the importing firm dependent on its suppliers. The terms under which international transfer of technology takes place are usually designed to ensure continued control of the technology by the licensing companies. Talking about turbo machinery, Pramod A. Paranji, a researcher with the UNDP, states,

> *"The licensing firm supplies only manufacturing drawings and drawing for tooling. They do not furnish design data; (. . .) if you want to modify a blade, you cannot because you do not have the data that went into the original design; . . .*

---

23   Ibid.

You can be sure that if a foreign firm gives you data, it will be out-dated. That way, you cannot make anything that will compete for its markets. Under a pure-licensing arrangement, it is hard to change specifications. If I want to change the steel in the turbine because I can get it from a cheaper source, the manufacturer will tell me he will not be able to guarantee the turbine if I do. If I am willing to pay, then he will let me know if the change can be made. This assumes my continued dependence . . ."[24]

Another difficulty is that of the inability of developing countries to assimilate transferred technology or their inability to adapt it to local conditions. A lot depends on the qualification of the labor force. Where it is trained in the sciences and the techniques, it may be easy for the economy to assimilate or adopt new technologies. But where such training is absent, assimilation will be difficult. Presently, the bulk of the workforce in most developing countries is unskilled, with the result that its ability to assimilate transferred technology is limited.

Even if there were resources to finance the transfer of technology and enough trained manpower to enable its adaptation to conditions in developing countries, there will still be one other major obstacle to the transfer process: the suspicion and concern that the transferor of such technology might lose control over its use. The exclusive use of a technology usually confers certain advantages to its owners. These advantages can be enjoyed only as long as similar techniques are not developed by others. With technological monopoly providing (on the long run) only a temporary advantage to its owners, its exclusive possessor will naturally tend to hold back its diffusion in order to preserve their advantages. In other words, they will want to prolong the life cycle of their secrets of production in order to maximize their returns. They will be interested in transferring the technology only if the expected profit

---

24   N. S. Buchanan and H. S. Ellis, *Approaches to Economic Development* (New York: the Twentieth Century Fund, 1955), 442.

from the transfer is likely to be greater than it would be if they exploited it exclusively. They will also be tempted (or even obliged) to transfer the know-how if there is a high probability that their exclusive control of it will be broken before long. From the possessor's point of view, the transfer of technology dictated by circumstances is only the lesser evil. It is a decision taken only when it becomes obvious that they cannot maintain effective control over the life cycle of their product: technology. In an interview to *Le Monde* newspaper, Jean-Paul Herteman, an executive officer in the French aeronautics company Safran, said,

> *"While the production of the most common parts can be carried out overseas, we produce the most sophisticated ones in France. We also have certain technical procedures which we want to maintain at home. The first reason for this is that the equilibrium of our economic model depends on after-sales service and spare parts. (. . .) The other reason aims at protecting our technologies because of concern for our national independence."[25] (MT)*

The very specific character of technology militates strongly against its free diffusion, and pecuniary compensation alone no longer looks sufficiently attractive to its owners. Buchanan and Ellis express the fear of competition that haunts would-be exporters of technology when they ask,

> *". . . Yet, if a nation divulges its superior techniques for political or other purposes, does it not run the risk that these very techniques will eventually be used to undercut its products in the world markets?"[26] (MT)*

For many developed nations, technology constitutes the main category of resources on which their economic superiority is based, and which enables them to maintain their lead. The economic rents

---

25   *Le Monde*, March 17, 2010, 5.

26   Buchanan and Ellis, *Approaches to Economic Development*, 442.

accruing to them as a consequence of their effective control over modern technology are so attractive as to compel them to be opposed to any real transfer of the latter. Indeed, their very economic survival depends greatly on their control of this category of products. It would be rather naïve to expect them to make public the secrets of their economic power. For to do so would be tantamount to relinquishing power and exposing themselves to danger. Nobody is willing to arm their enemies.

Entrepreneurship

Assuming the existence of resources in the required forms and in quantities sufficient to allow for their optimal combination, there will still be the problem of lack of entrepreneurship.

Simply defined, the entrepreneur is anyone who undertakes to invest, with the hope of making profit. Given the generally uncertain character of the future, whatever profit he makes is compensation for the risks he bears. In a very broad sense, therefore, anyone taking the risk to invest can be considered an entrepreneur. The local farmer who experiments with new farming methods or new tools with a view to improving his output is, in a sense, just as enterprising as the industrial investor. In both cases, they risk losing the resources they invest.

Profit making remains the primary objective of the entrepreneur. In the face of uncertainty, he will invest only if there is a chance, however small, that he attain his objective. The greater the chance, the more willing he will be to invest. Leaving aside all technical considerations, the choice of an investment project depends on two important factors:

- The degree of uncertainty involved
- The proportion of capital requirements relative to the investor's total amount of resources

The average entrepreneur in a poor country quite often finds himself in a situation in which both the proportion of his total amount of resources that an investment calls for and the risk of uncertainty are very high. In the face of such risks, his reluctance to invest is, to say the least, comprehensible. No other incentive, however great, will drive him to stick out his neck and invest in projects that hold no prospects for increasing his stock of values.

The presence of uncertainty and the extent of capital outlay, much more than the willingness to accommodate with poverty, account for the low propensity in the poor countries to innovate. Empirical evidence shows that even the poor in the poor countries are receptive of innovative ideas whenever these present a possibility for improvements in their living standards. When it became clear to people in the Third World that growing export crops improved their earnings, many of them quickly switched over to the production of these crops. That even among the poor, people are eager to finance the education of their progeny is evidence of their desire to break with J. Kenneth Galbraith's "equilibrium of poverty" and to refuse accommodation. Of course, investing in the education of one's children represents a certain degree of risk taking, but the consequences of a failure of such an investment are usually of little effect on the living standards of the family.

The inability or the unwillingness of the potential entrepreneur in the Third World to invest may be attributed to the accompanying high risk of failure. Needless to say that, especially in the industrial sector, they are the underdogs. Alone, they cannot be expected to gain ground against multinational corporations operating within their economies. Few artisan shoemakers, for instance, will be able to resist the assault of giant manufacturers like BATA. The latter, enjoying huge economies of scale and the benefits of many years of experience in management and marketing, will, without much effort on their part, outsell the artisans. Attempting to resist the advance of such giants would be suicidal to the small indigenous artisan in the Third World. Yet the financing of such a small project represents a greater sacrifice to the small entrepreneur than that represented by large-scale investments to the owners of big corporations.

The big investor thus stakes (proportionally) little but stands the chance of making great gains whereas the indigenous small entrepreneur throws his whole weight on the balance but still runs a greater risk of failure. The prospects of having to struggle for a share of the market with long-established, powerful competitors, therefore, serve as strong deterrents to would-be newcomers. Many potential entrepreneurs in the poor countries find themselves in just this situation. They are reluctant to invest what little resources they might have set aside, because they are unlikely to be competitive.

A breakthrough can best be made only if such small-scale investments are allowed to take place in an isolated environment. Indigenous small entrepreneurs need to be protected from the big (and usually foreign) corporations.

International Aid

Economists define foreign aid as any flow of capital to underdeveloped countries that is noncommercial, from the point of view of the donor, and that carries a very low-to-zero interest rate and that is repaid over a long period of time, if at all it is to be repaid. The recipients of foreign aid, generally, have no say in who gets aid, how much aid they get, and under what conditions. That remains the prerogative of the donors. It is obvious that in such circumstances, the donors are acting from a position of strength by virtue of the privilege they enjoy.

At a time when the world is facing a major economic crisis, some of the questions that may be asked are the following: Why don't the rich nations use all their resources to solve their own domestic problems first? Why do they have to transfer a part of these resources to other countries that may not be able to use them rationally? What is the purpose of aiding people in the periphery while those of the center are left to struggle alone with the adversities of an economic recession? Why doesn't charity, as the saying goes, begin at home?

The first answer we generally get when these questions are asked is that aid is distributed for humanitarian reasons. But as will be shown, there is more to it than just humanitarian feelings.

Aid as Political Instrument

In a bid to maintain their privileged relationship with former colonies, Britain and France have continued to grant economic assistance to these former dependencies. This is a sure way to maintain political leverage over the governments of these countries. Such aid is generally intended to fend off other nations (as was the case when communism was seen as a threat) who might seek to woo these countries. As Michael Todaro suggests, donor countries give aid primarily because it is in their political, strategic, or economic self-interest to do so.[27] The self-interest of the donor is the driving force behind the decision to grant or not to grant aid. The self-interests may be political, military, or economic.

Studies show that US aid to many African countries has declined since the collapse of communism.[28] Whereas there has not been any significant reduction in the levels of poverty in Africa since the collapse of the Soviet empire, one stands to wonder why Africa is getting less aid today from the United States than it did more than two decades ago. The coinciding of this reduction in foreign aid to this part of the world with the fall of communism has led some observers to say that with the threat of a communist takeover in Africa having disappeared with the demise of the Soviet Union, there is no more need for the United States to continue spending as if the threat were still there. It stands, therefore, to reason that the attention and all the money that were previously spent on Africa were intended not to fight poverty but rather as a means of fending off communism. Even the Marshall Plan, which enabled Western European countries to reconstruct after the Second World War, can be seen as intended to keep the communists from gaining ground in the region.

---

27   Michael Todaro, *Economic Development,* 5th ed. (New York: Longmans, 1977), chap. 15.

28   Marguerite Michaels, "Retreat from Africa," *Foreign Affairs,* vol. 72, no. 1 (1992/93), 93-108W.

Another very important reason for granting economic aid is to ensure political stability in the poor countries. It is feared that if people in the South are left in abject poverty and without any real hope of a change, a point might be reached where they would revolt openly, thus threatening the vital interests of the North. Expressing the need to preserve the interests of the North, Robert McNamara, former US defense secretary, said,

> ". . . *We are beginning better to understand that stability of relationships among rich nations is influenced by the stability of the institutions of the poor nations. And in the long run, the stability of the poor nations is a function of development . . .*
> *. . . The wealthy and secure nations of the world will realize that they cannot possibly remain either wealthy or secure if they continue to close their eyes to the pestilence of poverty that covers the whole southern half of the globe.*
> *(. . .) They will open their eyes and act, if only to preserve their own immunity from the infection."* [29]

Aid as Economic Catalyst

The decision to grant aid can also be motivated by economic reasons. A donor country might want to promote the export of its products. So it will grant aid in the form of loans to targeted recipient countries who are willing to buy the designated products. The donor country will thus earn interests from the loan as it is paid back, as well as profits from the sale of the designated goods. Whereas this arrangement represents an advantage to the donor country, it may be a disadvantage to the recipient country that might thus be paying a far higher price for the goods imported under this scheme than it would do if it bought them on the open market. Moreover, the donor country might require that

---

29   Robert McNamara, *The Essence of Security: Reflections in Office* (New York, Evanston, and London: Harper & Row, Publishers, 1968), 160-62.

the goods so purchased, be shipped, and handled only by the donor country's companies. Contracts to rebuild Iraq after the fall of Saddam Hussein were granted mostly to American companies.

The donor countries often use development aid to further their own interests in other ways. The *Brandt Report* clearly points out that the developed nations cannot expect continued economic growth without some form of participation by the South. But as the South is generally poor, the only way to ensure their participation is to grant them economic assistance. This suggestion is based on the argument that by transferring funds to the poor countries, they will be able to buy from the rich countries, which should keep the world economic machine running. The report states,

> *"For reasons which are partly historical, and partly based on the self-interests of donors and partly due to an inadequate understanding of the role of external resources in helping development, most of the official finance which developing countries get is earmarked for the purchase of capital goods from outside. In the initial stages aid was no more than an extension of credits which industrialized countries were providing to promote the export of their goods . . ."*[30]

This may be taken to mean that if there was no need to export capital goods, at least, a part of economic aid to the Third World would be without any purpose.

But not all aid funds are destined for the purchase of capital goods. An increasing proportion of it is being used for the purchase of consumer goods, with the consequent increasing dependence of the recipient countries on external sources of supplies.

Where attempts have been made by recipient countries to break the link between development-aid programs and imports from aid

---

30   Report of the Willy Brandt Commission, "North-South: A Programme for Survival" (London: Pan Books, 1980), 232.

donors, they have quite often provoked a negative reaction on the part of their benefactors. A recent report in the *International Herald Tribune* alleged that the United States government was considering stopping its aid program to Beijing because the Chinese government had failed to purchase as much grain from the United States as expected.[31] It turned out that wheat could be obtained on the open market at a cheaper price than that which the United States was asking from the Chinese. So here again, we can see that aid was tied to economic motives.

When foreign aid comes in the form of foodstuff, it may end up creating a habit in the recipient populations. The South Koreans, having got used to American food that they had come to know through aid programs, have continued to increase their imports of food from United States. At the same time, agricultural output in South Korea has continued to drop. It can be seen that the effect of such assistance is creating markets for products from the donor country.

By granting credit facilities, a donor country can also ensure future markets for spare parts for equipment bought with funds from the aid program. A further consequence of aid programs is that they compel recipient countries to import technical expertise from the donor to ensure the running or the maintenance of imported machinery.

Although it will not be reasonable to attribute the total value of the goods and services the Southern countries import to the fact that they receive development assistance from the North (after all, even those countries that do not receive aid still need to import those goods and services they cannot produce locally), it may be said that the aid recipient tends to give the priority of source of imports to its benefactors. All things being equal, Gabon will prefer to import from France while Israel will buy American products. Foreign aid may thus constitute only a small proportion of the development effort. But the leverage it confers

---

31   Michael Parks, "Slump in Grain Sales May Lead US to End Aid Program for China," *International Herald Tribune* (Paris), January 19, 1984, 3.

on its donors extends well beyond a fair proportion of their contribution. In a USAID discussion paper, it is claimed that

> *"AID has increasingly recognized that economic aid can promote development not simply by supplementing the host country's limited capital and technical resources but also by exerting influence on the country's policies and programs. As we have become more aware of AID's potential leverage role, we have experimented with techniques for exercising such leverage more effectively.*
>
> *In the long run AID's influence potential is much more important than its resource contribution. (. . .) Total aid from all sources has probably contributed roughly 20% of the total investments in developing countries in the past few years.*
>
> *The use made of the remaining 80% is much more important in accelerating growth than the use of aid alone. Furthermore, policies and procedures—import licensing arrangements, investment codes, marketing board pricing policies, power and transportation rate structures, tax provision, to name only a few—affect economic development at least as powerfully as the presence or absence of adequate infrastructure or technical skills. Successful efforts to influence macro-economic and sartorial policies are likely to have a greater impact on growth than the added capital and skills financed by aid."*[32]

Whether such influence serves the interest of the country to which aid is granted depends mostly on the extent to which the interests of the donor country are involved. Late senator Frank Church said in a 1972 speech on the Foreign Assistance Authorization Act that

> *"The Kennedy administration did make an effort to encourage democratic and progressive policies in countries to which it extended*

---

32   G. Ranis and J. Nelson, "Measure to Ensure the Effective Use of Aid," AID discussion paper no. 9, originally published in *Effective Use of Aid* (ODI, 1966), 85.

aid, but that effort was a failure. We failed because we had neither the ability to impose reform from outside nor the will to impose it from within. The one was simply impossible; the other went against the priority of our own interests as we conceived them. However much we may have wanted reform and development, we wanted stability, anti-communism and a favourable climate for investment, more. [33]

It is clear from Senator Church's speech that not all investments in the South engender economic development. Needless to say, a favorable and profitable investment (for the investor) is preferred to one which enhances development. American foreign aid is, therefore, being used here as a means of ensuring profit-making investments, sometimes even at the expense of economic development to the recipient country.

Eugene Black, former president of the World Bank, is also quoted as saying that

"Our foreign aid programs constitute a distinct benefit to American business . . . Foreign aid provides a substantial and immediate market for U.S. goods and services . . .
Foreign aid stimulates the development of new overseas markets for U.S. companies. [34]

Aid as an Expression Of Superiority

Foreign aid can also be considered an expression of the superiority of the donor over the recipient country. While it is reassuring to be in a position to donate to the poor, it feels even better to have an occasion to do so. For beside the influence that such an act confers on the donor, it also enables the donor to show that they are superior to the recipient. For rich nations, assistance (economic, technical, and military) to their

33   Extract from the speech by Senator Frank Church, reproduced by the *International Herald Tribune* under the heading "On the Limits to American Influence" (Paris), April 18, 1984, 4.

34   Quoted by H. Magdoff in *The Age of Imperialism* (New York: Monthly Review Press, 1967), 165.

poorer counterparts is just another form of Thorstein Veblen's *conspicuous consumption*.[35] And as the statement by secretary of state Condoleezza Rice after the 2005 tsunami disaster in Southeast Asia implies, some aid-donor countries may actually be looking out for occasions to make diplomatic gains when they extend aid. She said that Asia's tsunami disaster provided a "wonderful opportunity" for the United States to show compassion with relief efforts that reaped "great dividends" on the diplomatic front.

Consequences of Foreign Aid

Having stated in a nutshell the reasons why development aid is granted, let us now try to see whether it has been effective as an instrument of economic development. Some years ago, a British government paper outlined the purpose of development aid as, "To do what is within our power to help developing countries to provide their people with the material opportunities for using their talents, for living a full and happy life and steadily improving their lot."[36]

These objectives are, by all standards, quite reasonable. But to what extent have these or other objectives of this nature been attained by foreign assistance? What has been the price the developing countries have had to pay for such aid?

Again, it is difficult to attribute, with reasonable certainty, any portion of development achievements to foreign assistance for which the recipient has not suffered some negative consequences. On the contrary, it is easy to point out some of the negative effects on developing economies. Experience has shown that food-aid programs can discourage local agricultural activities. Where food is distributed free of charge

---

35   The concept of "conspicuous consumption" is advanced by T. Veblen in his well-known book *The Theory of the Leisure Class*. The widespread publicity given the decision to grant aid to the developing countries is a confirmation of Veblen's thesis. The purpose of such publicity is to impress the international public opinion. Political rhetoric is geared toward giving the impression that there is a one-way flow of resources, i.e., from the North to the South.

36   Quoted by E. F. Schumacher in *Small Is Beautiful: Economics as if People Mattered* (London: ABACUS, 1974), 136.

or at giveaway prices, the local farmers will be reluctant to invest in agriculture because of a lack market. If they do invest at all, it will be in the growing of export crops. But this, as can be expected, will only go to increase their dependence on foreign markets. In an article published in *Agripromo*, Vincent Rouze, a rural-development assistant in the Central African Republic, wrote,

> *". . . In the district where I work, I often hear farmers say: "Alone, we as Central Africans cannot develop our country. It is with the aid of the rich that we can develop." Recently, we witnessed a sad event which proved that foreign aid can also destroy a country . . . in the district of Boyo, for two consecutive years, groups of farmers have been struggling to sell their rice. Formerly, they sold only cotton. But the farmers expressed the wish to sell foodstuffs too. In 1980, an evaluation of the quantity of rice available for sale was made. Socada, the firm to whom they sell their cotton, came and bought 15 tons of rice from them. In 1981, another demand for the purchase of their stock of rice was made in Bangui. That also worked out well; the firm, Iaka, came and bought their rice. This time, the farmers had 45 tons to sell. People became interested in rice cultivation; and beside their cotton plantations, they grew more and more rice. This year (1982), the farmers of three districts went to the ministry to press for the purchase of their 100 tons of rice only to be told of rice donation from a rich country. The buyers don't want to purchase any more rice. They say the donated rice has invaded the whole market. 'If we buy your rice', the company officials questioned, 'to whom shall we sell it?' And there you are! The peasant's rice will not be bought . . ."[37] (MT)*

With their unsold stocks of rice, it is unlikely that these farmers would be willing to grow more rice in the future. Their efforts would

---

37   Vincent Rouze, *Agripromo* no. 45 (Abidjan).

certainly be diverted to the cultivation of cotton, an export crop for which there is a real market. But this is a market over which they have no control. Such aid programs, as we have just seen, can sabotage the efforts of an underdeveloped country to achieve self-sufficiency in food supplies.

As recently as March 2010, Bill Clinton, the ex-president of the United States, reportedly expressed regret for having implemented policies during his administration that damaged Haiti's agricultural capacity and its ability to feed itself. He described the policy as "an effort to free those places, . . . to skip agricultural development and go straight into the industrial era." What did that policy consist of? Well, it consisted of flooding the Haitian market with United States— subsidized foodstuff, especially rice, which ended up driving the locally produced foodstuff out of the market, thereby destroying local agricultural capacity.

If the Clinton administration really wanted Haiti to "skip agriculture and go straight into the industrial era," as he claimed, aside from helping to kill their agricultural sector, what did they do to encourage the creation of an industrial economy in Haiti? How could the people of Haiti have possibly embarked on an industrial adventure just as they were losing control of their ability to feed themselves? In pursuing such a policy, the Clinton administration's intentions might have been good, but it wasn't a completely innocent or disinterested policy option.

There were the American farmers with large stockpiles of farm produce who needed to find markets abroad. And those same farmers happened to constitute powerful electoral constituencies whose vote any American politician would want to woo.

Table 1: Haiti Rice Production and US Rice Imports, 1985 - 2000
In Metric Tons [5]

Year	Local Rice Production	US Rice Imports	Total*
1985	163,296	7,337	170,633
1986	163,296	24,683	187,979
1987	183,254	100,177	283,431
1988	166,018	54,465	220,483
1989	117,936	79,265	197,201
1990	116,122	112,987	229,109
1991	114,307	106,495	220,802
1992	112,493	126,885	239,377
1993	116,000	136,489	252,489
1994	100,000	87,766	187,766
1995	89,000	191,722	280,722
1996	115,000	167,116	282,116
1997	160,000	172,742	332,742
1998	101,300	183,678	284,978
1999	100,000	215,197	315,197
2000	130,000	219,590	349,590

Source: Department of Commerce, U.S. Census Bureau, Foreign Trade Statistics, Haitian Ministry of Agriculture, Food and Agricultural Organization, Bank of the Republic of Haiti

*This total does not include rice imports from countries other than the US. Haiti has imported small amounts of rice from other countries.

The emergence of a situation in which the granting of food aid becomes a necessity has another important consequence: it confers on the local authorities enormous power over the needy. The government of the aided country will be in a position to decide who benefits from the donation. They will distribute such unearned patronage only to those who support them even though these may not be the ones who deserve to be aided the most. The seizure in 1985 by the Ethiopian government of a six-thousand-ton food shipment from Australia that was intended for famine victims in Eritrea is an example of how a government can use the patronage that food aid confers on it to starve its own people.[38]

---

38   Editorial, *Washington Post*, reprinted in the *International Herald Tribune* (Paris), January 19-20, 1985, 4.

Such an instrument of internal politics would not be available to the government if the means of food procurement were not monopolized by any person or group of persons. In other words, governments will be unable to distribute such patronage if people were able to produce their own food.

Policy choices that encourage people to export on an empty stomach expose them to pressure from their own government— pressure that comes with the distribution of food received under aid programs.

The negative effects of foreign aid are not in any way limited to the agricultural sector. They are also present in the industry. The leverage that donors exercise on the recipients enables them to export goods to the latter at prices well above those that obtain on the open market. In the '60s, Pakistan was compelled to import railway equipment from France, which cost upward of 85 percent more than the price offered for equipment of comparable quality from West Germany and Japan.[39] (MT) The bane of tied aid is the artificial isolation of the recipient country from all other producers of a given commodity so that it is impossible to refuse to import at an exorbitant price. Beside the high cost of goods resulting from restrictive clauses in bilateral aid agreements, the receiving countries have to incur recurrent charges in the purchase of spare parts and the financing of repairs and maintenance work. The tying of aid has another adverse effect. It may prevent other developing countries from tendering for projects and competing for supply on an equal footing with donor countries. India, Brazil, and Turkey, whose capacity to export both technology and services has been increasing lately, may thus be unable to tender for jobs in other less-developed countries if such projects are financed through tied aid from the rich countries.

Foreign aid has been more instrumental in achieving its undeclared goals than it has been in achieving the publicly expressed ones. For example, more has been obtained in attempts to increase the Southern countries' dependence on international trade. Many African countries

39   Frères des Hommes, "A propos des élections présidentielles" (78000 Versailles, Jan. 10, 1981), 8.

that were once self-sufficient in food products have become increasingly dependent for food on the developed countries. Africa's net grain imports steadily went up from zero to twenty million metric tons between 1950 and 1983, and those of Asia jumped from six to seventy-one million tons during the same period. Meanwhile, Africa's exports of primary agricultural products increased tremendously.[40] The paradox is that the increase in the output capacity of these agricultural products is financed by foreign aid. The usual argument is that by increasing the export capacity of the agricultural sector of a developing country, it will be able to earn more foreign exchange needed to pay for its imports. But such investments in export production do not occur without the diversion of a substantial part of those resources that should otherwise have gone into the production of food for domestic use. Most important among these are land resources. Industrial agriculture, to be competitive, usually requires large areas of land. As the most fertile lands are used to produce for the export market, the peasants are driven to the less fertile ones. Their inability to produce enough food even for their own consumption can thus be explained. Brazil is a net exporter of agricultural products. Yet it has to import large quantities of food to feed its population. This is because it has concentrated on production for the export market at the expense of the home market.

After the cabinet meeting of November 7, 1974, a communiqué published by the French government claimed that thanks to French aid and technical cooperation, cotton output had increased tremendously in certain West African countries. The communiqué added that in seventeen years, export production had gone up fifteenfold in Mali, Senegal, and Burkina Faso (then called Upper Volta). It noted also that some difficulties arising from food shortages still persisted.[41] Needless to say, the bulk of the cotton produced in these countries is exported to France, which, in turn, is their chief supplier of imported food.

40   Worldwatch, "State of the World," quoted in the *International Herald Tribune* (Paris), April 21–22, 1984, 11.

41   *Le Monde* (Paris), November 8, 1979, 40.

The Western industrialized countries are in no way the only ones who use foreign aid as a means of guaranteeing their sources or supplies of primary commodities. The secretary for foreign trade in the defunct German Democratic Republic declared at a meeting of the Central Committee of the Communist Party that

"The GDR, up until now, supplied and installed at least 500 factories, pieces of equipment, workshops and training centres in developing countries. By so doing, we are creating conditions for long-term stable supplies of valuable raw materials coming from these countries."[42] (MT)

One of the officially stated objectives of certain international financial institutions is to foster development in the Third World. However, the actual policy priorities of these organizations differ greatly from the stated objectives. The IMF, for instance, was set up to promote orderly exchange conditions among nations. It was expected to do this by promoting international monetary cooperation by facilitating the expansion of international trade, leading to the maintenance of high levels of employment and income; by promoting exchange stability, maintaining orderly exchange arrangements; and by avoiding competitive depreciation of exchange rates. The IMF was also expected to provide adequate safeguards so that balance of payment problems could be solved easily.

For its part, the World Bank was charged with the financing of projects. It was set up to facilitate and to promote private foreign investments by means of guarantees and participation (. . .) and to promote trade and help with the balance of payments problems.

The activities of both organizations are financed by member states whose voting rights are determined by the size of their contributions. The power structure resulting from the distribution of voting rights is

42   Ibid., (Oct. 7-8, 1976), 4.

such that developed countries play a dominant role in the decision-making process. Some critics assert that these institutions take dictates from the governments of certain rich countries.

The question is whether these agencies actually and effectively serve the purpose of development. Available evidence suggests that their policies are aimed at goals other than development in the poor countries. The IMF and the World Bank are primarily concerned with stabilization in the recipient countries. They are especially interested in the safeguard of private property, the profitability of foreign investments, and the country's ability to pay back its debts. These considerations weigh more than any others in the decision to grant aid to a developing country. The social consequences of the choices of projects they support are of little importance. Indeed, where the attainment of social objectives conflicts with their stated economic goals, experience shows that priority will be given to the latter. According to a study by Teresa Hayter, stabilization programs (a major policy choice of the Word Bank) tend to reduce employment in both public and private sectors in recipient countries.[43] The Bank usually presses for a reduction in employment without considering the possibilities of alternative employment. A case in mind is that of Argentina from whom the World Bank extracted a promise for the military government to reduce employment in the railways by seventy thousand. No plans were made for alternative jobs for the would-be redundant workers. This shows the extent to which these institutions can go in trying to achieve the economic success of the projects they fund. No sacrifice seems too great. Not even the widespread unemployment caused by the measures they recommend seems likely to stop them.

International Trade

The existence of markets is obviously necessary for the expansion of an industry. Production will not be undertaken unless the producer is about certain to find buyers. Where the domestic market is too small

---

43   Teresa Hayter, *Aid as Imperialism* (England: Pelican Books, 1971), 160.

compared to the output capacity of a given industry, the export market usually provides an opening for the industry's surplus products.

As history has shown, international trade was of vital importance to the expansion of industry in England. We learn from Eric Williams's book *Capitalism and Slavery* that the triangular trade of the eighteenth and nineteenth centuries helped boost industrial production in England. For one thing, trade provided outlets for those surplus goods that England's domestic market could not absorb. And for another, by trading with other nations, the English were able to make huge gains that went on to finance further industrialization. Japan's economic expansion would have been less spectacular if there had not been export markets for its products. We can, therefore, draw the conclusion that for most countries, the export market is vital to economic expansion.

Economists claim that international trade is beneficial to trading countries. The doctrine of international specialization is based on the belief that if countries specialize in the production of those goods for which they enjoy advantages over others, the total output of goods will be greater than if each of them tried to produce all it needs for domestic consumption. But what proponents of international specialization fail to observe is that no guarantees exist to ensure an equitable sharing of the increased output. In the absence of such guarantees, there has been a marked deterioration in the trade terms of some countries in favor of the others. The terms of trade, which determine whether a country gains or loses in international transactions, depend on the bargaining position of the country relative to those of its trading partners. This position is, in turn, determined by several factors, such as the following:

    a. The nature of the products it offers for exchange
    b. The level of demand for such products
    c. The degree of the country's dependence on foreign trade
    d. The degree of diversity of both its products and its partners

It is obvious that the quantity of manufactured goods that is exchanged for a fixed quantity of primary commodities has been falling constantly. In other words, the terms of trade of exporters of primary products have constantly been deteriorating. In the 1960s, it took 7.5 kg of Tanzanian coffee to purchase a Swiss watch of a given quality; in the 1970s, a similar Swiss watch sold for more than 14.2 kg of coffee.

A country that exports easily perishable products has very little leverage over its trading partners. If its partners are manufacturers of durable goods, the chances are that they will dictate trade terms to it. For those countries whose export earnings are derived from the sale of only one or two primary products, their negotiating positions are even less enviable.

Trade between two countries may be likened to a zero-sum game, the net surplus of one being equal to the net deficit of the other. Where the game involves two equally developed countries (thus with comparable bargaining powers), there is virtually neither winner nor loser. In the North-South trade relations, there is a winner, the North, and a loser, the South. A country suffers no prejudice in exchanging a million euros' worth of goods for a million euros' worth of other goods. But a country that accepts (or is compelled by circumstances to accept) five hundred euros of goods in exchange for a thousand euros' worth of other goods it gives out suffers a prejudice of five hundred euros. I shall illustrate this argument with two simple examples:

1. Imagine a situation in which two equally developed countries trade with each other. In this situation, neither of them can expect to exert any undue influence on the other. So the goods that they exchange sell at their real market prices. If country A buys €1,000 worth of textile goods from country B to which it sells €1,000 worth of chemical products, neither of them makes any undue profits at the expense of the other.

2. Imagine another transaction involving a developed country D and an underdeveloped country U. Country D's bargaining position is better than that of country U. The former will almost

certainly tend to inflate the price of the goods it sells to the latter while preventing the latter from raising the price of its own goods. This will result in trade under unfavorable terms, with country U as the victim.

If, for instance, country D exports to country U finished goods worth €7,000 for the inflated price of €10,000 and imports from country U goods worth €12,000 for which it agrees to pay only €10,000, country D makes a net profit of €5,000 (€10,000 – €7,000 + €12,000 – €10,000), which is equal to the value of the prejudice suffered by country U.

In each of these cases, there results a trade balance between the trading countries. But while in the first case neither partner derives any undue profits, in the second case, country D obtains profits at the expense of country U.

In international trade (as, indeed, in all trades), each side aims at obtaining the best bargain possible from the other(s). As Botero puts it, a common way of enriching oneself at the expense of the others is through commerce.

At the time of the Industrial Revolution in England, the volume of that country's trade with Continental Europe might have been greater than that with the colonies. But the net profit (as has just been defined) she derived from its trade with the former was undoubtedly less than that derived from its trade with the latter. According to E. J. Hobsbawm, England's industrial economy grew out of her commerce, especially her commerce with the underdeveloped world.[44]

For international trade to be equally advantageous to both trading nations, certain conditions have to be met.

Some of these are that

- there must exist a situation of perfect competition;

---

44   E. J. Hobsbawm, "Industry and Empire," *The Pelican Economic History of Britain*, vol. 3 (England: Penguin Books Ltd.), 54.

- there must be full employment in all participating countries,
- there must be no trade restrictions of any kind and
- transportation charges must be negligible.

In the present situation in which international trade takes place, none of the above conditions exists. The outcomes of trade negotiations have distorted the market so much that there cannot be said to be even a semblance of perfect competition. Nor is there any economy that enjoys the luxury of full employment. All types of tariff and nontariff barriers are up today; transportation charges are not negligible, nor are they evenly earned by both trading partners. So some trading partners are bound to enjoy undue advantages in such imperfect market conditions. A country with a weak economy trading with another one whose economy is stronger and under conditions other than the perfect ones just enumerated above is likely to suffer a prejudice. It is evident that presently, the conditions under which trade takes place between developed and underdeveloped countries are far from conducive to fair trade.

Encouragement given to economic development in the South was primarily based on the argument that if productive capacities were increased there, they would be able to buy more goods from the industrialized countries. The South was encouraged to invest not only in the light industries but also, and especially, in the extractive sector. This stimulated growth in the developed countries where manufacturers of capital goods were eager to satisfy demand in the developing ones. The financial institutions were willingly cooperative. They granted loans to developing countries to finance their import of capital goods. Jean Dromer, president of the *Association Française des Banques*, describes the readiness with which commercial banks transferred funds to the Third World in these words:

". . . Finally, last but not the least, the banks too, were agreed. Their representatives were travelling the world in search of borrowers and

good projects to finance at the prevailing interest rate, but, especially, with commissions which allowed for considerable increase in the profits of the banking establishments."[45] (MT)

However, the enthusiasm that the Third World had aroused was short-lived. For as finished goods began to roll out of the newly installed factories in the South, it became clear to people in the North that it was necessary to take steps to check their inflow into their markets.

It may sound paradoxical to complain of trade barriers after having tried to show that trade between developed and underdeveloped nations was generally to the disadvantage of the latter. What should be noted is that these barriers exist only against manufactured goods and not against primary ones. Take, for instance, the case of Japan, which levies no import duty on cocoa beans but which charges 30 percent on imports of chocolate bars. The intention of Japan and other developed countries is to obstruct the import of finished goods (to which value has been added in the process of manufacture) and not that of raw materials. As Harry Magdoff points out, the United States places no tariff on imported iron ore. But a 20 percent duty is levied against sewing needles.[46]

The Structure of Protection

Degree of processing of goods	Average tariff imposed (as % of export value)	% share in the export of LDCs
1	4.6	71.2
2	7.9	23.8
3	16.2	2.9
4	22.1	2.1

Source: Bela Balassa: "The structure of protection", in UNCTAD. TD/B/C/C-2/36; 1970. Quoted by NR Richardson, in "Foreign policy and Economic Dependence" (University of Texas Press, Austin and London, 1978), p. 25.

It can clearly be seen here that the rate at which imports from the LDCs are taxed rises with the extent to which their products are

---

45   *Banque*, no. 436 (Paris, February 1984), 142.

46   Harry Magdoff, *The Age of Imperialism* (New York: Monthly Review Press, 1969), 165.

processed. Such trade barriers are, therefore, intended to check the inflow of finished goods. As primary products are processed, they take on more value, which makes them more expensive to importing countries and (what is even more important) which deprives the latter of job opportunities. Trade barriers of this sort have the effect of discouraging economic activities in developing countries and thus tend to compel these countries to specialize in the production of primary products only.

Governments of developed countries, however liberal they may claim to be, cannot turn a blind eye to the consequences of massive imports of manufactured goods from the South. It is their duty to protect the interest of their own citizens, a duty of which pressure groups constantly remind them. These groups are so well organized that their actions sometimes prove very effective in inciting governments to act on their behalf. French farmers frequently intercept truckloads of farm produce from other Common Market countries. (At one point in recent history, desperate American automobile workers were known to destroy Japanese-made cars, the import of which they accused for the decline in the American motor industry. The US Steel Corporation is constantly seeking government assistance to bar the inflow of steel products from developing countries. To heed their call, the US government would sometimes cut foreign aid to steel industries in the Third World or impose tariffs on imported steel products. That happened at least once during the George W. Bush administration.) At one time, the US government was even pressing for an agreement among industrialized countries to eliminate subsidies in export credits for steel plants in the Third World.[47] Obtaining a consensus on not granting credits for financing investments in the export industries is tantamount to trade restrictions. The principle of free trade is accepted by the rich countries only as long as it works in their favor. Whenever it is felt that it works against their interests, they take measures to protect their domestic markets. The Multifibre Agreement, for instance, was an invention of the developed countries

47   *International Herald Tribune* (Paris), December 27, 1983, 5.

who sought to protect their declining textile industries by obliging the LDCs to reduce their textile exports.

The Japanese are champions in the art. With their numerous specifications, they succeed in keeping out large quantities of manufactured goods that seek to enter their market. It is not just the government but also the whole Japanese nation that protects their market. The distribution network is controlled by influential commercial houses, such as the very famous Sogo Shosha, who are well-known for their economic nationalism. The Japanese consumer is conditioned, right from childhood, to buy and consume Japanese.

Protectionism today goes well beyond the physical restriction of foreign imports.

Manufactured goods from the South are often denied entry into markets in the North on the pretext that they are produced with very cheap labor. It is, however, interesting to note that people in the North do not question the cost of the labor that goes into the extracting of primary products that they import. Cheap labor ought to be considered an advantage to the LDCs, just as technical know-how is considered an important asset to the developed economies.[48]

Those who point out the positive effects of international trade on development usually pay very little attention to transportation charges. The net effects of international trade on a country's economy may not be correctly evaluated unless all the factors involved are carefully examined. One of them is transportation costs. High costs of transportation are not without consequences on international trade. It is in the interest of a trading nation to keep transportation charges low. Where this is not the case, economies of scale—resulting from international specialization—may be evened out so that the nation will not enjoy any advantages in

---

48   Froment-Meurice, director of economic and financial affairs at the French foreign ministry, asked, "… how can we continue to leave our markets open to products from developing countries where labour costs are much lower than ours?" Edgard Pisani, *La France dans le conflit économique mondial* (Paris: Hachette Littérature, 1979), 251. (My translation.)

trading with other ones. A study carried out by J. M. Finger and A. J. Yeats shows the following:

- Transportation charges tend to be higher on products exported by the LDCs than on products exported by developed countries.
- On the average, nominal transportation rates are, at least, as high as import tariffs.[49]

If transportation charges on imports from developing countries constitute an obstacle as great as the one that import duties add up to, they are worth being taken into consideration when discussing the net effects of international trade on the economy.

Losses Due To Freight Charges

International commerce between developed and underdeveloped countries is, by all standards, less beneficial to the latter than it is to the former. It has already been argued that by way of unfavorable trade terms, the LDCs give away to the developed countries more than what they receive in return. But not all losses incurred by these countries can be rightly attributed to unfavorable trade terms. There are also freight charges that they have to pay. More than 90 percent of the world shipping is controlled by the developed countries.

An underdeveloped country that uses its resources to produce for the export market with a view to earning the foreign exchange required to pay for its imports will have to incur transportation charges for its imports as well as for its exports. It may be more profitable for such a country, whenever it is possible, to allot a fraction of its resources to the local production of some of those goods that it will otherwise import. Not only will such a policy enable it to reduce its dependence on external sources, but it will also make possible substantial reductions in its transportation charges. Take, for instance, the case of Senegal, which

---

49   49 J. M. Finger and A. J. Yeats, "Effective Protection by Transportation Costs and Tariffs," The Quarterly Journal of Economics, vol. 40, no. 1 (Feb. 1976), 161-176.

grows and exports groundnuts (peanuts) to France. A reasonable part of its earnings from the export of this crop goes to finance the import of foodstuff. It will have to pay freight charges first for the export of its groundnuts and also for the import of foodstuff.

Let us imagine that the volume of its agricultural resources is such that if employed entirely for the production of export crops, it will earn foreign exchange over and above that required to pay for food imports. If, on the contrary, it decides to produce just enough food to meet home demand, there will still be left a stock of resources that may be employed in the production of export crops. The total freight charges incurred as a result of its trade with other countries will depend on the solution it adopts.

Let E represent the value of freight charges incurred in exporting only that part of Senegal's farm produce required to pay for its food imports. Let M represent the value of freight charges involved in exporting only that part of its farm produce required to pay for its import of manufactured goods. Let I stand for the freight charges involved in the import of food and F for the freight charges involved in the import of manufactured goods. If the country employs all its agricultural resources in the growing of cash crops for export with the aim of importing both the food and the manufactured goods it needs, the total sum of freight charges it incurs will be equal to $E + M + I + F$.

If, on the contrary, it produces enough food for its domestic market and employs the remainder of its resources to produce for the export market, the freight charges incurred for the acquisition of manufactured goods alone will be equal to $M + F$.

Whether these charges are wholly or partially incurred by the developing country, they will tend to diminish with the volume of trade.

From the table above, we can see that it is in the interest of the developing country to ensure that enough resources are employed in food production for domestic use so as to avoid the unnecessary shuttling of resources.

Effects of Specializing in Export Production

Proportion of Charges incurred by LDC	LDC specialized in Export Production while Importing Food (a)	LDC auto-sufficient in Food (b)
Freight Charges entirely paid by LDC	Freight Charges $= E + M + I + F$	Freight Charges $= E + I$
Only 50% of Freight Charges paid by LDC	Freight Charges $= (E + M + I + F)\,50/100$	Freight Charges $= (E + I)50/100$
X% of Freight Charges paid by LDC	Freight Charges $= (E + M + I + F)\,X/100$	Freight Charges $= (E + I)X/100$

By first ensuring self-sufficiency in food products, a developing country may obtain more value of both food and manufactured goods for a given quantity of resources than it would if it spent part of its foreign earnings on the food.

The losses that the developing country avoids by producing enough food for domestic use can be obtained by subtracting (*b*) from (*a*).

E.g., avoided losses = (E + M + I + F) – (E + I) = M + F or avoided losses = (E + M + I + F)X/100 – (E + I)X/100 = (M + F)X/100.

This demonstration is equally valid for most other articles that a country may wish to produce locally.

It may be argued that what is lost to the ones as freight charges accrues to the others as earnings on services rendered, so international trade actually helps create jobs in the transport industry. This is true, but it may be countered (and this is very important) that the earnings from freight services accrue to the developed countries that are in control of the shipping industry. Most developing countries are thus net losers in the exercise. It may be advantageous, therefore, for them to reduce their need for these services until such a time when they can produce them.

Self-Interest Imperatives

A man was sitting in a conference room waiting for the guest speaker to be introduced. Beside him sat another man accompanied by a four-year-old boy. The man with the little boy pulled out a wrapped donut from his lunch bag and gave it to the child, saying, "America runs on Dunkin' Donuts." Without a second thought, the other man said, in a tone that suggested he knew better, "No, America runs on credit."

Both men started to laugh; after which, the man with the little boy said, "We are trying to fix that now." He obviously was referring to the housing bubble that was rocking the United States at that very moment.

There may be some truth to the statement that America runs on credit, but actually, the United States of America and, indeed, the whole world runs on self-interest. And though scarcely ever mentioned in discussions on economic development, self-interest actually is a very important factor that needs to be included in the development equation. Even though mentioned by Adam Smith as an important factor in the pursuit of economic activity, it is amazing how the concept of self-interest has been all but *muted* by subsequent writers— especially, by students of economic development.

In the effort to protect and promote their perceived self-interests, those in privileged positions will always tend to act in a manner intended to, at least, maintain the status quo. And in doing so, they may impede the progress of others. Their action is driven less (if at all) by the desire to impede the others' progress than by the desire to maintain their privileged positions. Unfortunately, the one almost always engenders the other.

All economic decisions are generally based on self-interest considerations, which manifest as a response either to incentives or to threats to someone's well-being or comfort zone. They are the same self-interest considerations that Adam Smith identified as being behind the baker's desire to provide his customers with bread. They are equally the same self-interest considerations that are behind a firm's decision to relocate its production facilities from country A to country B. Similarly, a country's foreign-policy decisions are generally guided by what it considers its national or vital interests. In the case of a country, whenever national interests come in conflict with stated "national values," the former usually takes precedence over the latter.

Self-interests may be personal, as those of an individual, or collective, as those of a society or country. When it concerns a country, it is called national interest, and when it concerns a firm or business organization, it is termed corporate interest. Whatever we may term it, it is always behind most decisions we make. And since self-interest is thus involved, the decision makers usually seek to ensure that they (or those they represent) are not adversely affected by their decisions. Whether their decisions affect others adversely or not is only of secondary importance. Self-interest considerations can, therefore, lead to decisions which, while aimed at promoting one's own cause, may also lead to adverse effects on other people's causes or interests. And when the decision maker is thus compelled to choose between his or her own self-interests and those of others, it is always his or her own self-interests that are bound to prevail. There must be something in there for the decision maker, and all other considerations are secondary. Take, for instance, a company's decision to relocate its manufacturing facilities overseas where production costs are relatively lower than in the country where it is presently located. If that company successfully relocates, it is likely to see its profit margin improve. But in moving its production facilities to a new location, in pursuit of its self-interest (which, in this case, is a higher profit margin), it must lay off most of those who worked for it at the previous location. That, certainly, is good neither for its ex-employees nor for the community in which they live. The company owners may get away with such decisions only because they are the company's owners. And they are acting to promote their own interests.

Any nation that achieves the ability to wield much power places itself in a privileged position and enjoys enormous comparative advantage over others. It may use such power to create favorable conditions at home and, especially, abroad for the growth and expansion of its industries. It may invade or even just threaten other weaker nations with invasion to make them comply with its demands. Such invasion or threat of invasion is generally motivated by the powerful nation's desire to promote and protect its interests, considered in the broadest sense to include private commercial interests of its corporations. State agencies of such a power-wielding nation may thus be used to clear the way for private investment opportunities for its corporations or to obtain unduly favorable or lopsided commercial concessions from the targeted nation.

According to former US defense secretary Robert McNamara, the basic mission of the Department of Defense includes "supporting US foreign policy."[50] Which policy certainly includes creating favorable conditions abroad for American private business. The Department of Defense—in other words, the military—have, mostly, only two ways of acting in support of the country's foreign policy, namely, by taking military action and by threatening to take military action. So Secretary McNamara is saying that the military are there (in part) to go to war or to threaten to go to war in support of American foreign policy, which, it must be recalled, is determined by the country's national interests.

But the use of force is not the only means by which a powerful nation may promote and protect its interests. It may do so through the use of its diplomatic and political influence over international organizations. The increased threat by the United States of more economic sanctions against Iraq under Saddam Hussein allegedly caused that country to make ridiculously huge concessions to the United States, even before the 9/11 attacks and the countdown to the Second Iraq War. According to Susan Lindauer, who claims to have been a CIA asset, the secret service agency, working through what she calls back channels, had succeeded in wresting from the regime in Bagdad substantial commercial concessions, including the following:[51]

---

50   McNamara, *Essence of Security*, 121.

51   Susan Lindauer, *Extreme Prejudice* (2010), 76.

- The promise to grant US oil firms access to first-tier contracts for oil development
- The offer to buy one million American-made automobiles every year for ten years
- The promise to invest heavily in US telecommunications products and services
- The agreement to lean heavily on the purchase of US health care and hospital equipment and services
- The promise to allow all US corporations to reenter the Iraqi market in any postsanctions period at the level that they had operated prior to the First Gulf War.

Needless to say that those concessions, were they accepted and implemented, would have had far-reaching consequences for both the American and Iraqi economies. For one thing, they would have opened up a great market for American-made goods and services, and for another, they would have helped bring the Iraqi economy under US domination—an *unavowed* policy objective of any nation in a dominant position, which aims to increase or maintain its dominance over another nation.

This leads one to think that it is essential, in all relationships, for one to be in a position of strength—a position from which one can impose one's will on others. It is often necessary to be in a dominant position in order to successfully assert one's self-interests. Those who are in a privileged position are usually also in a dominant position. In the present economic relations between the developed and the developing countries, the former are in a position of strength, which enables them to impose their will on the latter or, may we say, to assert their interests against those of the latter. Acting in any other way would not be in their best interest, nor would they be acting in a way that conforms to normal human behavior.

We all have self-interests worth pursuing and protecting, and we all are, more or less, endowed with the ability to pursue and protect whatever we perceive as our self-interests for the moment. What distinguishes us from one another as individuals, groups, or nations is our ability to successfully protect or pursue our self-interests when they come in conflict with or are threatened by those of others. This ability is determined by the balance of power behind the respective contending self-interests. As should be expected, the strongest will always be the winners.

There is almost an inexhaustible array of tools with which an individual, a group, an organization, or a country can promote, assert, or defend what they perceive (rightly or wrongly) as their interests. They range from as subtle a technique as negotiating or persuading to as blunt a policy choice as going to war, and they include coercing, bullying, blackmailing, threatening the use of force, deceiving, using (or threatening the use of) physical or verbal violence, granting or withholding assistance, lobbying, employing and deploying economic hit men and jackals, cooperating or going into alliances with other companies or countries, engaging in corrupt practices, etc. Not all these tools are, however, available at all times to all. Nor are they all suitable for use in all situations. Those that are considered for use are determined by the given circumstances, the parties involved in a conflict, as well as the desired effects of their use.

Broadly speaking, there are two types of self-interests: short-term self-interests and long-term self-interests. These are not always compatible with each other. The pursuit of one may sometimes jeopardize the obtaining of the others. We are often tempted to pursue short-term interests to the detriment of long-term ones. The rush to invest in the Chinese economy thirty years ago was essentially driven by the pursuit of short-term interests. Investors from the West saw there huge opportunities for making quick money. In pursuing those opportunities, they ignored the potential for threat to their privileged positions, which an economically stronger China would come to pose. Granted, it was difficult for any of those interested in and capable of investing in China to ignore the promise of quick money when everyone else was rushing in. But thanks to Western technology, business methods, capital, and other inputs, the Chinese economy is today already posing a threat to the interests of many, even before it fully becomes of age. The West had thus chosen short-term interests (i.e., quick money) over long-term interests (unthreatened or secure privileged positions). And now, the genie being out of the bottle (at least, as far as Sino-Western economic relations are concerned), there is no turning back.

Self-interest concerns are always lurking in the background as we go about our decision making. They will allow us to be generous only if we do not hurt ourselves or whatever we perceive as our interests in the process. George Washington thought that ". . . with far the greatest part of mankind, interest is the governing principle; (. . .) and almost every man is more or less, under its influence."

Max Weber agreed with him when he said, "Interests (material and ideal), not ideas, dominate directly the actions of men . . ."

John M. Keynes was right in asserting, unlike what Adam Smith said, that the pursuit of self-interests does not always promote the common good. Sometimes it actually hinders the achievement of the common good. It may conflict with the goals of the common good, and when it so happens, the pursuit of the goals dictated by self-interest will prevail over the pursuit of the common good. For while the former is actively sought and defended by the decision maker, the latter is only hoped for at best. We know of no investors who would take up a project whose feasibility studies show that it will benefit only the common good to the exclusion of the investor's bottom line. By contrast, many an investor will readily carry on with a project even if it hurts the common good as long as it promotes the investor's interests and does not violate the law.

Every individual determines and defines what his or her self-interests are. What is included in that definition is not always legitimate or ethical. Those that are legitimate or ethical may be pursued openly, and those that are deemed legitimate or unethical are more likely to be pursued secretly, although with no less fervor than when pursuing the legitimate goals. Even when the self-interests being pursued are legitimate, it is not uncommon to use methods that are neither legitimate nor ethical. It is like engaging in a competitive sporting activity. In order to win—which, in this case, is the object of their pursuit—some competitors may, for instance, secretly take performance-enhancing substances or engage in some other unacceptable practices in order to have an edge over their rivals. This too happens in many economic activities where competition may be even more ardent and where there are even greater interests to protect. To have a competitive edge over others or to avoid competition in a given industry, an enterprise might find ways to set up or raise entry barriers high enough to keep potential competitors out. To wrench dominance of the browser market from Netscape, Microsoft decided to offer its own browser (the Internet Explorer) for free to Internet users, which made it difficult for Netscape to sell its Navigator. A study of the American telephone industry shows how AT&T fought long and hard to either destroy or absorb its rivals, which were called Independents.[52]

We do not really know the limiting factor. I think we can demonstrate, for instance, that in all probability, the presently underdeveloped countries are not going to develop. (. . .) If the whole world developed to American standards overnight, we would run out of everything in less than ten years.

—Prof. Kenneth E. Boulding

Behind the bureaucratic compulsion to control as much of the world political environment as possible, there lies a host of real human fears and drives, the fear of attack, the fear of losing influence and respect, the fear of falling from the pinnacle of power, the urge to make other

---

52   Tim Wu, *The Master Switch* (New York: Alfred A. Knopf, 2010), chap. 3.

societies conform to a perceived design, and the rationalized faith that the national interest and the welfare of mankind coincide.

*—**Richard J. Barnet***

CHAPTER III

Some Likely Consequences of Development

Not enough thought has been given to the consequences that development in the South would have on the world community. This aspect of the problem has been greatly overshadowed by the overwhelming attention paid to the study of the causes of underdevelopment. A look at these consequences may be of great importance in that it may help project the international atmosphere in which we are likely to find ourselves should the poor countries of the South become rich. By analyzing the likely consequence of development, we may be able to evaluate, with greater accuracy, the extent to which developed countries will be willing to contribute to development efforts in the South or, on the contrary, the extent to which they will be opposed to such development.

If economic development in the South is to mean anything, it should be able to provide a solution to the numerous problems of these countries. A developed country should be able to provide for most of its needs from internal sources or to control its external sources of supply. The developed countries of the West depend on the Third World for much of the energy they consume. But being in control of the shipping and the petroleum industries, they are in a position to ensure a near steady flow of oil to them. Most of the world's oil refineries are situated in the North, with the result that many developing countries (among them petroleum exporters) depend on the North for their supplies of finished petroleum products. The emergence of a developed South implies the eradication of this state of dependence. In that case, the South will no longer have to depend on the North for its defense needs, for instance. Another important consequence of such an eventuality is that the South will gain control of its own political destiny.

Perhaps the most evident of these consequences on the South will be an improvement in the general standard of living as characterized by increases in the supply and effective consumption of goods. Most of the manufactured goods consumed will then be produced locally, with increased use of locally available raw materials, labor, and technology. Whenever it is necessary, the countries of the South will import certain resources from the North. But such will have to be adapted to local conditions. It can be imagined that, in such circumstances, the South will require more of their natural resources for their own industries. That will invariably lead to a reduction in their export of primary products to the North. In short, the squeeze on the world's reserve of natural resources will be tremendous.

Paul W. Barkley and David Seckler have noted that

> *"If the rest of the World were to attempt to attain the present United States' standard of living (. . .), it would have to increase its output from twice to fully fifteen times the U.S. output."[53]*

According to Paul and Anne Ehrlich, statistics regarding requirements in raw materials show that raising the annual output of the rest of the world to United States' level would require seventy-five times as much iron, one hundred times as much copper, two hundred times as much

---

53   P. W. Barkley and D. W. Seckler, *Economic Growth and Economic Decay: The Solution Becomes the Problem* (New York: Harcourt Brace Jovanovich Inc.), 26.

lead, seventy-five times as much zinc (. . .) as is now being consumed in the world production.[54]

The problem is that under present circumstances, it is hard to see how the world, as a whole, can meet such demands for a reasonably long period.

Development does not only bring increases in per capita income; it also brings increases in output capacity. In a well- articulated development model, domestic supply should be able to rise with per capita income. In that case, the proportion of consumer goods that a country imports, relative to its total consumption or GNP, will tend to fall as development is achieved. Contrary to the widely held view, therefore, as the South develops, its need for imported goods will decrease. At the same time, its capacity to export finished goods will rise, so its actual volume of exports will be checked only by the North's capacity or willingness to absorb goods produced in the South. As can be expected, these countries of the South will acquire greater management skills. They will be in a position to set up their own capital-goods industries, build their own ships, and if need be, run their own transport lines. They will set up and run their own financial institutions. Thus their share of the global revenue accruing to the service industries will rise tremendously. There will also be a rise in their earnings from the ownership of technology by way of royalty. It is probable that their part in the overall value of world trade will increase. What is certain is that the pattern of world trade will change radically. The proportion of primary agricultural products in their overall export value will diminish whereas that of manufactured goods will go up. As the Southern countries take over the control of their economies, they will acquire greater bargaining power and will be better placed to negotiate for more favorable terms of trade. Economic aid from the North will lose all relevance as the South becomes able to fend for itself.

The net effect (on the North) of the South's emergence as an economic power will probably be negative. Not only will the North

---

54   Paul and Anne Ehrlich, *Population, Resources, Environment: Issues in Human Ecology* (San Francisco: W. H. Freeman & Co., 1970), 61-2.

be confronted with the problem of shortage of raw materials, but its markets will also be flooded with finished goods from the South. The example of China's emergence as an economic power and its effects on the world marketplace is there for all to see.

Let us suppose, for the sake of argument, that the Southern countries became as developed as those of the North. There would surely ensue a scramble for the available stocks of raw materials. A study group of the Massachusetts Institute of Technology produced a report for the Club of Rome. The report claimed, among other things, that

> *"Added to the difficult economic question of the fate of various industries as resource after resource becomes prohibitively expensive is the imponderable political question of the relationship between producer and consumer nations as the remaining resources become concentrated in more limited geographical areas. Recent nationalization of South American mines and successful Middle Eastern pressures to raise oil prices suggest that the political question may arise before the ultimate economic one."*[55]

In a recent news report on the PBS television program *NewsHour*, it was reported that because of the growing demand for rare earth metals at home, China, where about 95 percent of the world's rare earth supplies are now mined and refined, has started scaling back on their export. Claiming that these metals were needed for home use, Zhang Anwen, a Chinese mining official, reportedly said,

> *"Foreign countries should calmly and logically think about this and develop their own mines for their own needs. Our resources are diminishing. And we need these minerals for our own use."*[56]

---

55   E. F. Schumacher, *Small Is Beautiful: A Study of Economics as if People Mattered* (London: ABACUS, 1974), 100.

56   "Rare Earth Minerals Scarcity Worrisome for Growing Tech. Sector" (June 14, 2010), www.pbs.org/newshour/bb/business/jan-jun10/metals.

As can be imagined, the emergence of a developed South will not only affect the economic life of the North but will also threaten its political power. This obviously will result in a shift in the balance of power. The Northern countries' chances of dictating policy to the South will be reduced. In other words, the South's ability to resist political pressure from the North will increase. The United States has fewer problems today dictating policy to Kenya, for instance, than it has dictating it to France.

As the South moves upward (economically), the leverage that the North has over it will tend to diminish. Those instruments of foreign policy designed to perpetuate dependence will become obsolete. And since power is relative, as that of the South increases, that of the North will decrease in a corresponding proportion. While this represents a triumph for the South, it will mean a decline for the North.

There is every reason to believe that in the event of development in the South, at least some of the consequences mentioned here will be observed. The emergence of countries like Japan and South Korea as industrialized nations accounts for at least part of the current economic crisis in Europe and North America. The growing capacity for the South to export manufactured goods is no doubt causing concern in the North. According to a study by Jean Lemperiere, the South's share of manufactured goods imported into United States went up from 10.6 percent in 1966 to 28 percent in 1982. Taken as a whole, the South is today the greatest supplier of manufactured goods to the United States.[57] Considering the volume of US imports from China at the start of the twenty-first century, this is even truer today than it was in the '80s.

Given that the share of finished goods in the South's total export value accounts for more than 50 percent today, it will be erroneous to continue to consider this group of countries as primarily exporters of raw materials and importers of finished goods. Although consumer goods still account for the greater part of these countries' total export value, the share of capital goods is steadily increasing. Meanwhile, the

---

57   Jean Lemperiere, *Le Monde* (Paris), June 5, 1984, 20-21.

value of manufactured consumer and producer goods imported by the South continues to fall. This fall cannot be attributed entirely to the current world economic crisis. For despite the crisis, many countries in the South have achieved unequalled growth rates. African economies have been growing at annual rates as high as 5 percent in recent years. Similar growth rates have also been observed recently in South American countries. It is at least plausible to state that some of them have become self-sufficient in certain categories of finished goods. Furthermore, as they acquire increased export capacities, they become able to supply other developing countries, thus reducing the latter's need to import from the North. The result is the reduction in the developed countries' export of finished goods to the South.

AMERICAN EXPORTS OF MANUFACTURED GOODS TO THIRD WORLD COUNTRIES

(In billions of dollars).

	1981	1982	1983
Exports to Latin America	31.5	23.2	16.9
Exports to Asia	14.8	16.3	16.2
Exports to the Middle-East	10.7	11.2	9.5
Exports to Africa	4.5	3.9	2.7
TOTAL	61.5	54.6	45.3

Source: OECD and US Dept. of Commerce

In the light of the foregoing, it can be said that the thesis of "mutual" economic interests of both the North and the South will remain plausible only as long as the present status quo is maintained. If, by some miracle, the South became developed, the present arrangement would dislocate. While such a development would tend to reduce the South's dependence on North, the latter would, on the contrary, find it hard to reduce its own dependence on the former. The vacuum created as the South achieves autonomy will not be easy to fill. And the notion of mutual interests would be replaced by that of mutual antagonism. Such antagonism was expressed by Professor Ansiaux in the following terms:

"The issue of Japanese competition (. . .) is an obstacle (. . .) to the establishment of tolerable trade relations among different nations of the world." (MT)

Indeed, since 1936 when this declaration was made, events have continued to show that Ansiaux's apprehensions were not totally unfounded. Between 1936 and 1981, Japan's trade pattern changed greatly.[58] (See table below.)

EXTERNAL TRADE OF JAPAN

	Imports		Exports	
	Primary goods	Finished goods	Primary goods	Finished goods
1913	56.6	37.0	45.1	45.4
1929	66.7	24.4	43.1	49.3
1933	75.5	17.4	27.0	64.0
1971	67.9	28.5	4.8	93.7
1981	74.1	22.1	2.4	96.3

Figures are % of total import or export values.
Source: 1913, 1929, 1933, Paul Berryer, "Le commerce extérieur du Japon", in Bulletin de BNB; 1934-2, pp. 201-206 : 1971, 1981, Ministry of Finance, Tokyo; Summary Report on Trade of Japan

The inability of the Northern economies to do without those of the South was implied by Marie Schlei, the minister of cooperation in former West Germany, when she said that

---

58   Prof. Ansiaux, (*Bulletin de la BNB* [1936-2], 37-40) quoted by Eric Verreydt in "Le péril jaune se porte bien-un siècle de grogne européenne à l'égard du Japon," *Revue bimestrielle: Reflets Perspectives de la Vie Economique* (Tome XXII-Mai, 1982-2), 139-150.

"The dependence of our economies on the export market is very great, (. . .). Over the last few years, it has grown vis-à-vis the developing countries. Today, 22% of our exports go to the Third World. Roughly a million jobs depend directly or indirectly on these exports. The importance of developing countries as an export market will increase even further, for the level of saturation for capital and consumer goods will remain unattained for a long time to come. The required condition is the raising of the buying power and the level of demand in these countries. The only way of achieving this is to reinforce the integration of developing countries in the international economy and in the long run, that will be profitable to both parties."[59] (MT)

A representative of the EEC is also known to have declared that

"The Third World countries are our best customers: they absorb 38% of our exports, whereas the United States absorbs only 13% (. . .); the more the Third world becomes developed, the more they will be able to purchase our technology. Just as a trader sells more in a well-to-do area than in a poor one."[60] (MT)

The least that can be said of the latter statement is that it lacks consistency. For while it is easy to explain why the United States buys so little from Europe, it is rather difficult to understand how demand by the Third World for European goods and technology will continue to grow with economic progress. If there was a correlation between a country's position on the ladder of development and the level of its imports of European goods and technology, then the United States, which is by far more developed than the Third World countries, would be importing more (and not less) than developing nations import from Europe.

---

59   Interview given by Marie Schlei, West Germany's minister of cooperation, in *Le Courrier* (ACP-CE), bimestrial no. 46 (Brussels, Nov-Dec 1977).

60   Frères des Hommes, "A propos des "Elections Présidentielles," 6.

A trader's sales volume depends not only on the area in which he or she operates but also on the sort of articles he or she has to offer. If he or she offers to the well-to-do the sort of goods that are usually consumed by the poor, his or her turnover is likely to be less than it would be if he offered the same goods to people in the poor areas. Should the developing countries become capable of producing their own technology (a plausible supposition, given that it is both consequential of and compatible with development), the need to import such technology from developed countries will be reduced.

A feature common to the last two quotations is that their authors consider the Third World only as a potential market for finished goods from the North. No thought is given to the South's need and increasing capacity to export finished goods to the North.

Placing the North-South relations in the setting just imagined, the struggle for development in the South becomes comparable to the situation on a unique lifeboat that would sink if overloaded. The likelihood of the boat sinking is greater if all those who seek to get on board are allowed to do so. Those who, by chance or by virtue of their personal effort, get on board first would do all within their powers to maintain the boat afloat. This would invariably include taking measures aimed at preventing too many people from getting on board. But the others, who obstinately believe they can survive only by getting on board the boat, would not be deterred by the warnings of those already rescued. The struggle for survival would then oppose the ones to the others.

The scenario imagined here is not completely unrealistic. Clinton P. Anderson, former US secretary of agriculture, once declared that

"Some people will have to be deprived of food (. . .). We are in the situation of a family which possesses a number of puppies: we must decide which ones have to be drowned."[61] *(MT)*

---

61   *Fortune* (May 1946). Quoted by Mark Spits in "Violence silencieuse: famine et inégalité," *Revue Internationale des Sciences Sociales*, no. 4 (1978).

Experts have frequently drawn the attention of the public to the possible dangers caused by the advent of the South. After having analyzed the progress made by the South, Jean Lemperiere came to the conclusion that

". . . in the best of hypotheses, (. . .) time does not work in favour of the industrialized countries. They, at least, ought to take this into consideration and to prepare themselves for a world in which, though still maintaining several advantages, would lose their hegemony and some of their privileges."[62] (MT)

If, as has been noted, development in the South threatens the privileges of the North, then the latter could be expected to take preemptive measures to preserve those privileges. Such measures would likely include resistance to development in the South.

The average human being or group of human beings tends to defend their acquired advantages whenever these are threatened. European farmers, especially the French, quite frequently take steps to prevent the entry of farm produce into what they consider their home markets. Their action, illegal as it may be, is quite justifiable if we consider that their material well-being depends on their ability to market their products. All other things remaining unchanged, the ability to sell a product reduces as the market becomes saturated.

It is also because of the desire to protect vested interests in the European shipbuilding industries that the Association of West European Shipbuilders expressed their deep concern over South Korea's planned expansion of its shipbuilding industry.[63]

---

62   Jean Lemperiere, "Les échanges Sud-Sud : Progrès et Contradictions," *Politique Etrangère*, no. 2 (Paris: June 1981), 399–400.

63   *Financial Times* (London, April 1, 1982). It is rather paradoxical that the North, who are strong proponents of economic liberalism and who are opposed to all forms of central planning, should want to dictate investment policies to other nations. Such an attitude does not conform to the principles of liberalism, which demand that the market alone (should) determine where to invest and in what proportions.

Shipbuilders and shipping authorities in the North/West have every reason to be anxious. Between 1970 and 1977, the developing countries' share of the world-order book jumped from a mere 1.4 percent to nearly 16 percent. That of the Western industrialized countries fell from 96.5 percent to 77.9 percent during the same period.

World Order Book 1970 – 1977 ('000 GRT) Year End

Year	Third-World	%	OECED	%
1970	1.112	1.4	75.783	96.5
1971	2.020	2.4	79.869	95.5
1972	2.287	2.6	82.418	95.3
1973	4.834	3.8	122.037	94.7
1974	6.985	5.8	111.786	92.6
1975	7.482	9.1	72.881	88.5
1976	6.017	10.7	47.050	85.0
1977	5.851	15.9	18.609	77.9

Source: Liyod's Register of Merchant Shipbuilding Returns. Quoted in "The Emergence of the Third World Shipbuilding". N° 61, March 1978. Published by H.P. Drewry Ltd, London

Although the reason for which most Third World countries set up their own shipping industries is noneconomic, the consequences of their emergence in the shipping world are not negligible, hence the anxiety of those whose interests seem threatened.

The desire to remove all that threatens one's privileged position is a trait common to all people or groups of people, irrespective of their origins.

On his return from a visit to India, the French agronomist René Dumont recounted,

"As I advised this landlord to increase the land under irrigation, he shouted: 'Certainly not! That would ruin me. There would be much more land to cultivate; so, my earnings from rents would fall. There would be work for everybody; so, I'd have to pay higher wages to my

labourers. There would be more grain on the market, so I'd have to sell at cheaper prices.' This man has vested interests in misery. He makes more gains with the usury and sharecropping systems than with increases in production.'[64] (MT)

In Burkina Faso (formerly Upper Volta), the government once set up a grain bank. This semipublic organization was set up to ensure a fair distribution of grain in order to prevent speculation by petty traders who bought it at a very low price from zones with an excess crop harvest and sold it at extremely exorbitant prices in other zones where there were shortages. A major problem of the grain bank was that of the insufficiency of funds, for it did not receive subsidies from the government. Attempts to obtain loans from local commercial banks failed because the traders, who provided the bulk of the funds deposited with the banks, threatened to withdraw their money if the latter lent to the grain bank.[65]

The interests of both the Indian landowner and the petty trader in Burkina lay in the misery of the local population. Whatever privileges they enjoyed and whatever influence they had over the poor would vanish if the latter were allowed to make substantial improvements in their living standards and if they became economically independent of the rich. Such improvements would represent a threat to the interests of the privileged, whence the readiness of the latter to put up resistance.

In the mid-1980s, the Nigerian government expelled some two million unwanted immigrants from the country. The brutality with which the expulsion was carried out was decried by many across the continent. But what could not be decried was Nigeria's duty toward its citizens. In defending what might be termed its citizen's interests, the Nigerian government was, indeed, defending its chances of retaining power. Yet the decision to expel illegal aliens from the country was against the spirit of the so-called African hospitality. Such a decision

---

64   René Dumont, "Frères des Hommes," *Bulletin Trimestriel*, no. 51 (Versailles: Printemps, 1983), 3.

65   Frères des Hommes, *Témoignages et Dossiers* (Versailles, February 1983), 30-31.

finds justification only in the assertion that people tend to defend their interests and advantages (earned or unearned) whenever these are threatened. At the time, many Nigerians claimed, without any real proof, that their economic difficulties were due to the massive influx of people from neighboring countries. Their expulsion was decided as a means of recovering some of the lost ground.

Three decades ago, in an attempt to reduce Senegal's dependence on imported wheat, the *Institut de Technologie Alimentaire* (ITA), a Dakar-based public agency, undertook to experiment on the baking and the distribution of bread containing a mixture of wheat and millet. Technically, the experiment was a great success. But it had to be called off. Marie-Thérèse attributed the abandonment of the project to the vested interests of those involved in the wheat-import trade. She wrote,

> *"Many people were not interested in having wheat gradually replaced with millet. In Senegal, the food industry is largely foreign-controlled. All but two of the firms in the food business are in the hands of foreigners—the flour mills, as well as the bakeries."[66] (MT)*

The urge to resist attacks or to protect acquired privileges is in no way a recent phenomenon. Evidence of this can be found throughout human history. As early as the nineteenth century, the emigration of technicians and the export of certain machines from England to Continental Europe were prohibited. The reason for such a policy on the part of England was easy to guess. All successful transfer of technology to the rest of the world was thought to represent a potential threat to the economic interests of England. If other countries achieved even a modest level of development, England's dominance of the world would have run the risk of being challenged. It was, therefore, advisable to prohibit such transfer in order to prevent such an eventuality.

---

66   Anne-Marie Cap-Impe, "Sénégal, les leçons d'un échec," *Jeune Afrique Economie*, no. 34 (Paris, March 1, 1984), 48-9.

The countries of the North would acquiesce to development in the South only as long as it did not conflict with their (the North's) interests. But development, as it is now conceived in the South, is likely to remain in open conflict with the North's economic and political interests.

If asked to choose between development in the South (with all the attendant negative effects on the North) and maintenance of the status quo, with all the security it provides for the North, we can be sure that an overwhelming majority of people in the North will opt for the maintenance of the status quo. Again, this would be the obvious choice of most people who find themselves in a similar situation. This attitude, this logic of self-interest, goes a long way in explaining why, despite the world's capacity to produce enough to ensure food security for all in the world, widespread hunger still subsists in many parts of the world. It explains, perhaps, more than any other single factor, why we may never achieve John M. Keynes's *universal abundance.*[67] The privileged will continue to throw all their weight on the balance to preserve, if not augment, their advantages. They may accept to aid the less privileged only if their interests remain unaffected as a result of their aid.

The development aid that the rich nations hand out to the poor ones has both long-term and short-term effects. From the donors' point of view, development aid is essential in that it helps create markets for their manufactured goods in the aided countries. But the ultimate goal of development assistance, as viewed and wished by the South, is not just to help increase their import capacity but rather to also make it possible for them to develop their own productive capacities.

Supposing that the resources received under aid programs were used in a rational manner so that the expected results were achieved, the consequences on the North, as had already been stated, would be grave. And the North does not at all seem prepared for such an eventuality. Rather, it seems easier for the North to prevent, or at least delay,

---

67   *Essays in Persuasion: Economic Possibilities for Our Grandchildren* (England: St. Martin's Press, for the Royal Economic Society, 1972, 326. John M. Keynes predicted the attainment of universal economic abundance within a hundred years.

development from happening in the South than to face its consequences when it does happen. The advent of the so-called Newly Industrialized Countries (NIC) on the world economic scene has caught the North quite unprepared and has left them quite uneasy. The early stages of the industrial development of the NICs coincided with the massive importation of capital goods from Europe and North America. But as the NICs became increasingly industrialized, the net flow of industrial and other goods to these countries diminished. Such are likely to be the long-term consequences of development in the entire South.

The question here is not that of whether the NICs' industrial achievements resulted from the aid they received from the North but rather that of the adverse effects that their rapid growth has had on the Northern economies. The Northern countries are unlikely to be happy to have other South Koreas and other Taiwans mushrooming all over the globe. Therefore, since economic aid is intended to help the poor countries achieve development, it cannot be compatible with the North's long-term interests. Aid policies aimed at improving agricultural output in the South will not receive the blessings of those European and American farmers who export to these countries, because if self-sufficiency is achieved there, the need to import food will decline.

The rich countries of the North, who talk of a moral obligation to encourage development in the South, may thus be trapped in a dilemma. Either they assist the poor countries in their struggle for progress and face the likely outcome or they abandon their aid programs and run the risk of losing both their credibility and their political leverage.

The political motives for interfering with the development process in the South have quite often been stated in no uncertain terms. Senator Hubert H. Humphrey once said,

"I have heard this morning that people may become dependent on us for food. I know that was not supposed to be good news. To me, that is good news, because before people can do anything, they have got to

Between nations, development is a scarce "commodity." And scarcity can be the basis upon which domination and exploitative relationships are grounded. If the hungry submit readily to political manipulation by those who feed them, then the poor and the underdeveloped can also be expected to accept political domination in the hope of receiving food aid. In a like manner, those who seek to obtain the cooperation of other countries would only be too glad to learn that the latter are dependent on them. And the best way of perpetuating such dependence is to obstruct development in the dependent countries.

As machines—a product of technology—increasingly displace humans at the workplace, there'll be greater unemployment. The fact that in certain countries some people will continue to hold two or even three jobs at a time just to make ends meet does not mean that there will be enough work to go round. (By the way, if someone has to hold more than one full-time job to survive, it means either he or she is living above his or her means or is engaged in the wrong kind of profession.) As a consequence of further development, the workweek will likely shorten again in order to give more people a chance to earn a living. For nearly three decades now, certain European countries have been experimenting with a shorter workweek. This has not shown much promise in reducing unemployment, because of productivity gains (a consequence of development) that continue to reduce the amount of resources—especially labor—needed for a given level of output. So in the end, development may prove incapable of meeting one of its objectives (that of providing opportunity for all those who wish to work to do so) as was defined in chapter 1 above.

---

68   H. Humphrey, *Hearings* (Senate Agriculture and Forestry Committee, 1957), 129.

It may be said that technology—which promotes development and which, in turn, is promoted by development—comes at a price measured in more than just money. One of the ways in which that price comes is the environmental risks that accompany technology use. In a model developed by Allan Schnaiberg, showing the relationship between environmental problems and quantitative and qualitative aspects of technology used in production, it is shown that environmental problems increase with the degree of modernity of the technology used.[69]

We learn from this model that all technology, at some level of production, becomes harmful to the environment. But the level of production at which a given technology becomes harmful to the environment varies with the degree of sophistication of the technology. The less traditional or the more modern the technology, the lower the level of production at which the technology becomes a problem. In other words, for a given level of production or a given quantity of application of technology, modern industrial technology causes more environmental problems than does traditional technology.

Therefore, as we move away from traditional methods of production and into modern methods of production, the bar above which the application of technology begins to create environmental problems continues to drop. So in using modern technology, if we maintain the same level of production as we did with traditional technology, we will be inflicting greater harm to the environment than we did while using traditional technology.

As we go along, population problems will become more acute. Thanks to modern medical science and technology, life expectancy will continue to increase. The natural occurrence of population-control epidemics have been greatly reduced. Some thinkers have already drawn our attention to impeding problems of overpopulation as they are proposing that there be some kind of measures to population growth

---

69   Allan Schnaiberg, *The Environment, from Surplus to Scarcity* (New York / Oxford: Oxford University Press, 1980), 116.

rates. The Indian government of Mrs. Indira Gandhi tried it once. China is presently tackling the problem head-on by limiting to one the number of children per family.

Given the projected population growth and the diminishing known stocks of resources, there is going to be a squeeze at some point—a squeeze that might lead to armed struggle over access to scarce resources. Writing in the French daily, *Le Monde*, economics professor Joseph Brunet-Jailly draws our attention to the risk of armed conflicts over scarce resources when he says,

> *. . . But, in principle, the recourse to military actions of this type cannot be ruled out; the millennium report on the environment does not exclude the scenario of "order [imposed] by the use of force. That says it all. »[70] (MT)*

Robert Heilbroner, in responding to his own question as to what will be the attitude of the rich nations toward the industrialization of the poor ones, hinted at the possibility of war. He wrote,

> *"The mechanism of resolution will have to be political, perhaps military—where, we should remember, all the trumps are not in the hands of the West."[71]*

So once again, as the South gears up to achieve development, we are reminded that one of the consequences of its becoming developed could be the risk of war. The question then is, Who wants war if it can be prevented—even at the cost of development to others?

> *But beware! The time for all this is not yet. For at least another hundred years we must pretend to ourselves and to everyone that fair*

70   "La mondialisation, une chance pour les pays pauvres," *Le Monde* (Paris), April 13, 2005, 14.

71   Robert Heilbroner, *21st Century Capitalism* (New York / London: W. W. Norton & Company, 1993).

is foul and foul is fair; for foul is useful and fair is not. Avarice and usury and precaution must be our gods for a little longer still. For only they can lead us out of the tunnel of economic necessity into daylight.

—*John M. Keynes*

When US and European Union trade negotiators jointly proposed that instead of the OECD lowering these production subsidies poor countries might shift to other activities, I felt they had crossed the line beyond which the normal diplomatic act of lying for your country becomes too shaming to accept.

—*Paul Collier*

When we talked about the power of the little guys, I had to exercise a great deal of restraint. I knew what none of them could possibly know, that the corporatocracy, its band of EHMs, and the jackals waiting in the background would never allow the little guy to gain control.

—*John Perkins*

America, like Britain before her, is now the great defender of the Status Quo. She has committed herself against revolution and radical change in the underdeveloped world because independent governments would destroy the world economic and political system, which assures the United States its disproportionate share of economic and political power . . . .

America's preeminent wealth depends upon keeping things in the underdeveloped world much as they are, allowing change and modernization to proceed only in a controlled, orderly, and nonthreatening way.

—*Richard Barnet*

CHAPTER IV

Resisting Development

Having determined that the rich and the privileged, in their desire to defend what they perceive as their interests, may, sometimes involuntarily, act in ways that impede the progress or jeopardize the well-being of others and having also determined that, by virtue of the very privileges they enjoy, the privileged are often in a position to affect (negatively or positively) by their actions the lot of other people, let us now look at how they might act in the face of perceived threats to their interests. To focus more directly on our subject, we may ask the following questions: What is the likely attitude of the North toward the eventual development of the South? As has been suggested, are they in a position to successfully oppose development in the South? What evidence is there that they are deliberately standing in the way of development in the South? And what would be the rationale for obstructing development in the South?

The desire to come to the assistance of the South has, from time to time, been expressed by some world leaders. But so too has been expressed (albeit in a more muted manner) the intention to withhold such assistance.

President Harry S. Truman, in his inaugural address of Jan. 20, 1949, in which he announced his now-historic Point Four Program, said, among other things,

". . . Fourth, we must embark on a bold new program for making the benefits of our scientific advances and industrial progress available for the improvement and growth of underdeveloped areas.

More than half the people of the world are living in conditions approaching misery. Their food is inadequate.

They are victims of disease. Their economic life is primitive and stagnant. Their poverty is a handicap and a threat both to them and to more prosperous areas.

For the first time in history, humanity possesses the knowledge and the skill to relieve the suffering of these people."[72]

The writer Gregg Easterbrook expresses his desire to see the "defeat of global despair" in these words:

"Two generations ago, the nations of the West took on as their challenge the defeat of fascism. One generation ago, the nations of the West took on as their challenge the defeat of communist tyranny. (. . .) The nations of the West should take on as their next historic challenge the defeat of global despair."[73]

As will be argued in this chapter, it takes more than just the availability of sufficient quantities of resources to provide for the needs of all. Indeed, ever since that address by Harry Truman, the knowledge and skills needed to defeat despair and relieve mankind of suffering have not stopped growing and accumulating. So with all such goodwill, with access to so much capacity, why can't despair be defeated?

A young mother was travelling on a bus in the city of Paris. She was accompanied by her two kids. The elder of them, a boy, was about five years old while his kid sister, who kept crawling all over her mother, was no more than three.

---

72   Harry Truman's 1949 inaugural address.

73   Gregg Easterbrook, *The Progress Paradox* (New York: Random House, 2003), 284.

The city bus on which they were travelling took a turn around the corner of a block only to reveal a full view of the Eiffel Tower. The young mother, in an attempt to quiet her two kids, called their attention to the majestic *Tour Eiffel.*

"Oh, look at the Eiffel Tower over there," she said to the children, who immediately stopped playing and turned to look at the tower.

As they drove past the monument, the young boy turned to his mother and asked, "What would happen if the tower were to fall?"

"No," replied his mother, "it cannot fall."

"Let us just suppose," urged the young boy, "that it fell. What would happen?"

"No," insisted the mother, "it just cannot fall."

"What if a very strong wind blew and knocked it down? What would happen?" the boy said with a hint of impatience in his voice.

The mother, as though to reveal a secret to her young son or just to give him an answer she was not sure of, lowered her voice and said, "It cannot fall because some people we cannot see from here are working all the time to make sure it does not fall."

The boy turned to take another look at the monument, not quite convinced by what his mother had just said.

Resistance to development in the South today can be likened to the one that Western European countries experienced when their governments struggled to establish the welfare state or to the current struggle in the United States over health-care reform. And as Gunnar Myrdal says,

"Inasmuch as the movement toward the Welfare State carried the promise of equalization of opportunities and a broader sharing of the national welfare . . . , it placed financial burdens on the privileged classes and threatened their freedom to use their power of wealth as they pleased. (. . .)

*Particularly in the earlier stages of the reform movement, it was
natural, indeed, that those with vested interests mobilized political
power to protect themselves and tried to resist the launching of the
social and economic reforms."*[74]

Development in the South today holds the promise of greater
equalization of opportunities and of limiting the power of the North. So
similarly, we can expect those of the North to naturally resist it, which,
of course, they might actually be doing in more or less subtle ways.

Referring to one of those subtle ways of resisting development in the
South, John Perkins, a confessed former economic hit man, writes,

*"When we talked about the power of the little guys, I had to exercise
a great deal of restraint. I knew what none of them could possibly
know; that the corporatocracy, its band of EHMs, and the jackals
waiting in the background would never allow the little guys to gain
control. (. . .) In fact, I understood that the stranglehold of the global
empire was growing stronger, despite OPEC—or, as I suspected at
the time but did not confirm until later, with OPEC's help."*[75]

In a recollection of a 1941 conversation between British prime
minister Winston Churchill and US president Franklin D. Roosevelt
that took place aboard a battleship, Elliot, Roosevelt's son, reported that
Churchill, in response to Roosevelt's remarks about British Empire trade
agreements that were supposedly perpetuating backwardness in India,
Africa, and other British colonies, said,

*"Mr. President, England does not propose for the moment to lose its
favoured position among the British Dominions. The trade that has*

---

74   Gunnar Myrdal, *Beyond the Welfare State* (New York / Toronto / London: Bantam Books), 137-138.

75   John Perkins, *Confessions of an Economic Hit Man* (New York: Plum Books, 2006), 89.

*made England great shall continue, and under conditions prescribed
by England's ministers."[76]*

In an article published in the *Guardian* under the caption
"Technology Transfer to Developing Countries Is an Impossible Dream,"
Cath Bremner, while not saying why, hinted at the reluctance of owners
of technology to divulge it. She wrote,

*"For a start, governments don't own intellectual property, companies
do. Getting them to surrender it is no easy task."[77]*

Just as the little boy in Paris had his doubts about why the Eiffel Tower
could not be imagined to topple over someday, the reader too might have
reason to question the sufficiency of present-day economic development
theories in explaining persistent underdevelopment in the South. But
thanks to a growing body of writings and other pronouncements, we may
be in a position to suggest that there exists what might be called *resistance
to development.* We can no longer ignore stories told of people who,
with the blessings of international institutions and others, are overtly
or covertly engaged in schemes intended to get developing countries to
make investments that not only do not hold any promise of meeting
their needs but also make those countries perpetually dependent on the
developed countries. When we read stories of how the IMF objected to
Ethiopia's early retirement of its loan with an international bank, we are
bound to question the end to which the IMF was counselling Ethiopia.[78]
Similarly, Erik Reinert relates that after half a century of industry building
that went from 1940 to 1990, the share of agriculture in Mongolia's
economy had diminished from 60 percent to 16 percent. But persuaded
by consultants from the World Bank and the IMF, Mongolia opened up

---

76   Erik S. Reinert, *How Rich Countries Got Rich and Why Poor Countries Stay Poor* (New York: Public
Affairs, 2008), 169.

77   Cath Bremner, www.guardian.co.uk/environment/cif-gree/2009/dec/09/ technology-transfer.

78   Joseph Stiglitz, *Globalization and Its Discontents* (New York: W. W. Norton & Company, 2003), 30.

to globalization or what the author calls the de facto Morgenthau Plan. And within four years of that opening up (between 1991 and 1995), the author says the country's industrial sector had shrunk by more than 90 percent.[79] Upon reading such a story, one is bound to wonder what the so-called Washington Institutions thought they were doing. Were they promoting development or resisting it? Obviously, judging by the outcome in this particular case, like in more than a few other cases, it can be safely said that they were resisting development.

When Dr. Ron Hira and Dr. Anil Hira, in their book *Outsourcing America*, worry about *"how to prevent the better [American] technology or know-how from diffusing quickly to the developing countries,"*[80] they are thinking about how to prevent the developing countries from acquiring such technology. So they are thinking about standing in the way of development in those countries. Resistance to development is rooted in the very pursuit of self-interests to which, as a matter of fact, we are all entitled. But just as we are usually quick in claiming our right to the pursuit of self-interests and also in pointing out how the pursuit of these self-interests is important to the market economic system, let us be as quick too in recognizing the strong inclination in us to defend those same self-interests whenever threatened. Let us equally be quick in admitting that in defending what we perceive as our self-interests, we may be brought to prevent others from pursuing their own self-interests when seen as in conflict with ours. Adam Smith's perfect market conditions—if ever they existed—have since disappeared and with them his invisible hand that governed the market to ensure the upholding of the public good while individuals pursued their self-interests. They have been replaced, it must be admitted, with the grossly imperfect market whose hand is not so invisible. One only needs to follow this new hand to find out who is manipulating the new, imperfect market— and to what end. Lawrence Summers's appointment by the Clinton administration to the

79   Reinert, *How Rich Countries Got Rich*, 174.

80   Ron Hira and Anil Hira, *Outsourcing America* (New York / Atlanta: American Management Association, 2005), 190.

presidential economic council was opposed by environmentalists because he was said to be in favor of Third World industrial development in spite of the risk of environmental degradation, and he had reportedly said,

"Nobody should kid themselves that they are doing Bangladesh a favour when they worry about global warming. Poverty is already a worse killer than any foreseeable environmental distress."[81]

Indeed, in a 1991 World Bank internal memo, talking of "Dirty Industries," Lawrence Summers had also reportedly said,

"Just between you and me, shouldn't the World Bank be encouraging more migration of the dirty industries to the LDCs [Less Developed Countries]? I can think of three reasons; . . ."[82]

And he went on to give three reasons to support the migration of "dirty" industries. On the one hand, the developed world still needs some place where they can always go to dump their dirty industries. (Remember Union Carbide in Bhopal, India?) If the whole world were to develop, there would no longer be any such place. So let there continue to be underdeveloped areas, and that's what Summers's memo implies. On the other hand, environmental activists in the developed countries who oppose industrial development in the South do so not because they hate (or love) the South but because they care more for the environment in which they live, and they fear that development in the South (even in Bangladesh, which is thousands of miles away from the United States), while improving the living conditions of the people there or while bringing dirty industries to their backyard, will eventually engender a deterioration of the environment in the developed world in which the

---

81   Gregg Easterbrook, A Moment on the Earth (New York: Penguin Books USA, 1995), 588. (See Summers' World Bank Memo of Dec. 12, 1991; Subject: GEP.)

82   Lawrence Summers's World Bank Memo of Dec. 12, 1991.

activists live. It is still out of self-interest that they may be opposed to a certain kind of industrialization, whether at home or abroad.

The Two-Pronged Strategy

The North's attitude toward development in the South is expressed through what might be termed the two-pronged strategy. It is a strategy by which the North seeks to remain credible in the eyes of the South as well as to remove all that threatens its (the North's) interests.

The first objective is attained by creating and maintaining the impression that development in the South can be achieved only with the help of the North and (what is even more important) that the North is doing all it can to assist in the development effort.

The second objective is attained by undermining development in the South inasmuch as an eventual emergence of the South as a developed entity would leave the North economically worse off.

For such a strategy to be efficient, much publicity must be given to those actions meant to enhance credibility while those intended to stand in the way of development must be concealed as much as possible. Political rhetoric is geared to give the impression that there is a one-way flow of resources, i.e., from the North to the South. No mention is made of the northward transfer of other resources such as primary products, returns on foreign investments, capital repayments, interests on loans, as well as payments for transferred technology and other resources.[83]

Inscriptions such as "GIFT OF THE PEOPLE OF GERMANY" or "DON DE LA FRANCE" normally form an integral part of the packaging in which donated food and other goods are presented to the recipients. A multinational that overcharges its clients in the Third World or sells them its secondhand or obsolete equipment is unlikely to reveal that piece of truth. This discretion is necessary because if it is suspected

---

83   Pierre Pflimlin, the erstwhile president of the European Parliament, expressed a similar view when he declared that too much was being said about aid to the Third World but not enough about the developing nations' contribution to the developed nations' prosperity. (See interview in *Le Courrier: ACP-CE*, no. 90 [Bruxelles: Bimestriel, Mars-Avril 1985], 54.)

that a force is acting to inhibit economic development in the South and, especially, that such a force is being deliberately applied, either the struggle for development will be abandoned or alternative strategies will be sought for by the South.

The components of the two-pronged strategy, contradictory as they may appear when considered separately, are actually complementary. They are two aspects of one and the same scheme that aims at preserving the North's enviable position. Pursuing only one or the other of these policies will (from the North's point of view) be counterproductive. If the countries of the South were given to doubt the ability or the readiness of the North to help with their development problems, if they were to stop looking up to the North for deliverance, they (the Southern countries) would try to develop through their own effort. And if their own efforts proved a way of ensuring a certain degree of economic independence, they would strive to make these efforts more efficient. In which case the economic relations between the North and the South would be severed or greatly reduced. That means that there would cease to be domination of the South by the North. (Since the concept of domination presupposes the existence of a constant flow of goods, information, ideas, etc., between the dominant and the dominated.) The North would then run the risk of losing it privileges vis-à-vis the South, for as has already been observed, preserving these privileges requires that it maintain its dominance over the South.

If, on the other hand, the South were aided to achieve development, its control by the North would disappear. And as in the previous case, the North's privileges would be lost, too. This dual strategy is the most apt to create and maintain the right climate for the preservation of the North's privileges. For while making the North look credible and while giving the South hope, this strategy makes the obstruction to development in the South not just possible but also effective. Any departure from this strategy could only be limited both in time and space. And such departures are usually politically motivated. Such was the case with American economic aid to the Southeast Asian countries that enabled them to industrialize. Such, too, was the case when, on the eve of French Guinea's independence, the French horridly left the West African country, taking away everything they had brought into the colony. They even ripped off and took away line phones. Sékou Touré, the new president of soon-to-be-independent Guinea had turned down General de Gaulle's invitation to remain under the French-led Communauté Française d'Afrique. The French thought that by rejecting their offer, the Guineans were fighting against any influence that the ex-colonizers might have sought to maintain over them. Whereas the first of these two departures allowed the Southeast Asian countries to progress economically, the second one removed what little hope there had been for development in Guinea. Industrialization was encouraged in South Korea, Hong Kong, Macao, Taiwan, etc., only because it was thought to be the best way of stopping the communist advance in the region. In the same way, the Marshall Plan (under which the United States granted economic aid to Western Europe at the end of the World War II) was inspired less by the generosity of the Americans than by their desire to hold the communists in check.

Where the threat of a communist takeover is minimal and the escape from domination is unlikely to be propelled from within, the Northern countries' desire for development will be minimal.

The success of the two-pronged strategy is, perhaps, easy to explain: Development having been achieved in the North, it takes little effort to persuade people in the South that it is possible to repeat the exercise. Underdevelopment is then presented less as a consequence of an ongoing conflict of interests than as a primitive stage in the natural evolution toward development. People in the South are then given to believe that to achieve development, all they need to do is imitate the North. The success achieved by South Korea and other ASEAN countries is held up as evidence that, with the help of the North, the South too can become developed.

But the industrial success achieved by these countries has another important consequence that must not be ignored. Its effects on the Northern economies incite them to increase their resistance to the industrial development of the other countries, for the relative success of the ASEAN countries has not left the North totally indifferent. The current wave of protectionist measures adopted against goods from these countries as well as the call for them to increase their imports from the North can be seen as an expression of the North's embarrassment at their success. This embarrassment will naturally lead them to question the wisdom in aiding other would-be competitors.

The two-pronged strategy finds expression in every aspect of international economic relations: in the exchange of goods and services, in the transfer of technology, in overseas investments, in foreign aid, etc. Not that the transfer of technology or the granting of aid are in themselves bearers of the germ of domination. Indeed, when allowed to play a neutral or impartial role in international cooperation, they can contribute greatly to development. But when used as instruments of the two-pronged strategy, they take on a pervasive character, for as all neutral instruments, they are open to abuse or manipulation by those who control them. Presently, it is the North, not the South, who controls them.

Economic integration provides an ideal atmosphere for the flow of goods and services between nations. The greater the occasion for economic intercourse between the North and South, the greater are the chances of abuse or manipulation by those in control. No wonder, therefore, the North's eagerness for integration with the South.[84]

Two agents are principally responsible for the integration of the South into the world economic system:

- The governments of developed countries
- The multinational corporations (MNCs)

---

84   Ibid, no. 46, Nov–Dec 1977. Marie Schlei, the West German minister for cooperation expressed the desire for increased integration of the Southern economies into the world system.

Of the two groups, the more instrumental in the process seem to be the MNCs. Their part in the international transfer of goods, technology, and other resources is predominant. Governments may enter into agreements providing for the transfer of technology, for instance, but in the final analysis, it is the MNCs who decide where to transfer their technology and under what conditions. The bulk of economically exploitable technology is controlled by them, not their governments. It is they who, above all, are in a position to decide the fate of developing nations.

A very obvious way for the government of a developed country to drag an underdeveloped one into its economic sphere is by invasion or war. The subdued country then becomes obliged to cooperate with the invader. The trade ties that have developed between the United States and Taiwan, South Korea, and Japan since the World War II owe a lot to the occupation of the latter countries by American troops. Such was the case with the economic relations between the defunct USSR and East Germany or Poland, which, until the late 1980s, could still be considered as occupied by Russia.

Economic aid is another of those instruments used to foster integration. During the colonial period, the colonies were considered integral parts of European empires. Economic activities between the colonial power and their overseas dependencies could not be hindered in any way.

But this was not going to be the case after decolonization. The newly independent states, as was expected, questioned their continued involvement in the European economic sphere under prevailing conditions. It then became necessary for the retreating colonial masters to institutionalize economic aid as an instrument of foreign policy in order to continue to play an influential role in the economies of their former dependencies.

Economic aid that is made conditional to imports from the donor country encourages integration. So too do trade agreements that provide for preferential treatment or for higher-than-world prices for the exports of a developing country. The trade agreement between ex-Soviet Union and Cuba, under which Cuban farm produce were bought at relatively higher world prices, is an example of measures that governments of developed countries can take to ensure the integration of underdeveloped economies into theirs.

Trade remains the main instrument through which the multinationals control or influence economic development in developing countries. Investing in these countries presents an important occasion for them to influence the choice of trading partners as well as items of trade. If the quest for political influence is high on the priority scale of a multinational (as is sometimes the case with MNCs investing in the Third World), then the choice of investments will be such as to increase its role in the host country's foreign trade and, more particularly, its trade with the MNC's country of origin. It will invest in raw materials or primary goods production or in intergraded production. This is especially the case with the mining industry where the various stages of material processing are designed to take place in different countries. Guinea's alumina was reduced into aluminum in Cameroon. The American company Kaiser insisted with the Ghanaian government that only the last stage of the long process of bauxite refining take place in the country. And for that, it had to bring alumina from abroad. Bauxite was extracted and beneficiated in Jamaica and was converted and reduced into aluminum in the USA and Ghana, respectively. By so doing, Ghana was deprived of a chance to develop its known deposits of bauxite, which was the original purpose for the Volta Dam project.[85]

By spreading out its activities in different countries, the MNCs succeed not only in avoiding control by the authorities of the countries in which they operate but also in influencing their trade patterns. Until recently, most petroleum refineries were situated in developed countries—far away from oil fields in Africa and the Arabian Gulf area.

---

85   G. Lanning and M. Mueller, *Africa Undermined* (England: Penguin Books, 1979), 429-35.

Investment by multinationals also tends to be in production that exhibits constant technology change and/or large infrastructure needs. In many cases, most of the capital goods required have to be imported, with the risk of an excessive outflow of resources by way of overpricing, head-office charges, and shipping and handling charges. Again, the mining industry presents a good example. In Liberia before the civil war, mining companies operated their own railway lines, which ran between the minefields and the seaports. Such investments, as can be expected, produced very little linkage effects on the local economy. Their capital-intensive nature made it unnecessary for them to hire local labor.

Sometimes, the host country is obliged to commit a substantial part of its resources to the provision of costly infrastructure (special port facilities, dams, or railway lines), which may be useful only to the multinationals.

The multinationals' strategy usually consists of trying to place themselves in such a power position as to make it impossible for the authorities of the host country to dislodge them without hurting the economy. If a company accounts for a substantial part of government revenue or of total export value or if it gives employment to a great number of people, it will be difficult for the government to interfere in its affairs without threatening the very interest it seeks to protect. Once in such a position, the foreign companies may at anytime blackmail the government by threatening to stop operating in the country. The authorities would then find themselves in the uncomfortable position of having to make costly concessions in order to persuade the multinational to stay. If the host government stubbornly stands in the way of the MNC or if it threatens the interests of the latter, the MNC that has gained such a strategic position in the local economy can make life difficult for the host government.

One company that once attained such a strategic position (at least, in one country) was the American fruit conglomerate, the United Brands Co. The country was Costa Rica. That company was threatening to cease its activities in the banana plantations on the Pacific coast. The measure of that company's influence on the Costa Rican government can be imagined if we reckon that the country relied on banana production for the crucial sum of almost forty million dollars a year in concessionary payments and taxes.[86] What was more, about fifty thousand Costa Ricans depended, in one way or the other, for their living on the Pacific coast plantations. The French oil giant Elf was another of the MNCs with influence on so many Third World countries.

As far as MNCs go, Elf was in a class of its own. Ostensibly, the company was created to ensure France's energy sources. But in reality, it was far more than just an ordinary oil company. As it turned out, it was a front for French secret services in Africa. Elf's creation coincided with the beginning of Africa's decolonization. So as France was publicly relinquishing control over its dependencies in Africa with one hand, it was secretly taking it back with the other hand through the revolving door that the newly created front company, Elf, provided. Although there already existed another oil company (Total-CFP) of which the French state was a stakeholder, General de Gaulle still went ahead and ordered the creation of Elf because he wanted a company that was wholly owned by the state and which would be its '*arme seculaire*' in the oil business. The company soon grew to be the kingmaker in many of the African countries in which it operated. Nothing of any significance (political or economic) could ever happen in those countries without Elf being involved. The revenue it amassed from its oil operations provided it the wherewithal to have great influence over the governments of those countries.

In a long interview published in book form, Loïk Le Floch-Prigent, ex-general manager of Elf, said, among other things,

> *"Elf is not only a petroleum company. It is a vehicle for parallel diplomacy intended to maintain control over a certain number of African States, especially at the moment of decolonization. (. . .)*

---

86   "US in Dilemma on Costa Rican Bananas," *International Herald Tribune* (Paris), January 15, 1985, 5.

Elf was created to operate as a petroleum company—which it has done successfully; but it also acts as an extension of the State, so that France's policy on Africa can be in line with its (France's) interests. (. . .) Let's say that the general manager of Elf is both the GM of a petroleum company and the Cooperation Minister number 2. And it is because this company had both political and diplomatic objectives in Africa that it has always funded secret service operations. (. . .) a number of covert operations were organized to maintain political stability in certain countries . . ."[87]

In another interview published in the French weekly *Express*, the ex-GM of Elf Oil Co. said further,

"It is thanks to Elf that France maintains a presence in francophone Africa and extends it to other countries. So is it in Gabon, where Elf appoints Bongo. It is true for Congo, (turned Marxist for a time and still under the control of Elf). It is also true for Cameroon where president Biya ascends to power only with the help of Elf, in order to contain the Anglophone community of this country;"[88] *(MT)*

Explaining his role in Africa as the GM of Elf, he said in the same interview that his role included

". . . Paying attention to the presence of France in Cameroon and in Chad. It is the reason why Elf joined the Chad oil consortium alongside Exxon, in replacement of Chevron—a consortium that is going to define the route for the pipeline across Cameroon; and my role is to discreetly persuade the Americans to make the pipeline take the francophone part of Cameroon; -to maintain the Savimbi-Dos

---

87   Loïk Le Floch-Prigent, entretien avec Eric Decouty, le cherche midi editeur, *Affaire Elf: Affaire d'Etat* (Paris, 2001), 54.

88   *L'Express* (Paris), December 12, 1996), 66 and 68.

---

*Santos equilibrium in Angola so that there would be no winner and
so that they will be obliged to come to agreement.[89] (MT)*

It is worth noting that the war in Angola, in which hundreds of
thousands of innocent people died, lasted twenty-seven years while
French gunrunners joined others in supplying arms to both sides in the
conflict—just to maintain the equilibrium. It is also worth noting that
the pipeline referred to here was originally planned to run from the oil
fields in Chad to the deep seaport of Limbe in Anglophone Cameroon,
but thanks (perhaps) to Elf's "discreet persuasion" of the Americans, it
was rerouted to the coastal town of Kribi.

According to the Swiss author Jean Ziegler, the Nigerian civil strife
that started as a secession and ended up in what came to be known as
the Biafran War was instigated by French secret services acting on orders
from General Charles de Gaulle. After the new Nigerian leader Yakubu
Gowon abruptly ended the oil concessions his predecessor had granted
Elf Oil Company, the French general reportedly got angry and thought
he needed to come to the "defense of France's strategic interests." A
few months later, there was an attempted secession by the Ibos in the
southeastern part of Nigeria. This was followed by a civil war that lasted
thirty months during which some two million Nigerians were killed.
That civil strife, which was nothing other than a proxy war between
France (for Elf) and Britain (for Shell-BP), ended almost immediately
after the contending oil companies were reconciled at a meeting on Jan.
12, 1970, in Paris, France, at which they signed an agreement on how to
share Nigeria's oil resources.[90]

Since these countries have been under the influence of foreign powers
who seek primarily to assert the strategic interests of the countries they
represent, isn't there a chance that their efforts at achieving development
could be thwarted or undermined by these occupying foreign powers if

---

89   Ibid.

90   Jean Ziegler, *La haine de l'Occident* (Paris: Éditions Albin Michel, 2008), 188-191.

such development were perceived as capable of threatening the interests of these powers? The civil wars in both Angola and Nigeria disrupted the development process in those countries and set them back by several years just because some other persons were asserting what they considered their strategic interests.

The undue influence that such foreign oil companies exert on certain developing countries can be further understood if we consider the share in those countries' total merchandise exports that petroleum products represent. According to WTO international trade statistics for 2008, they represented 99 percent of Angola's total merchandise exports and 92 percent of Nigeria's.

Oil Export Value as % of Total Export for Given Countries

Country	Export in $	% of Total Export
Algeria	$77,822.000.000	98.1
Angola	$66,437.000.000	99.0
Cameroon	$2,653.000.000	61.0
Gabon	$4,585.000.000	84.1
Ivory Coast	$3,628.000.000	35.9
Ngieria	$74,281.000.000	92.0

Source: WTO, International Trade Statistics, 2009, Table II.22

Meanwhile, interference in the affairs of foreign companies is made difficult, if not impossible, by their use of technology of which only they have the mastery. That then serves as a pretext to hire large numbers of technicians from industrialized countries. Attempts by ex-president Mobutu of former Zaire Republic (now called Democratic Republic of Congo) to take over control of the activities of Union Minière were frustrated, among other things, by the company's announcement that a thousand technicians had asked to leave the country.[91] Needless to say that the presence of those technicians was essential to the stability of the company's mining operations.

It may well be true that corporations are guided not by geopolitics but by profits, but in the final analysis, corporations might be better advised to side with the government of their respective home countries. It is true that corporations control technology, but the transfer of such technology to other countries may be restricted by the government, making it sometimes necessary for a corporation to meddle in geopolitics. To obtain the green light to deliver two Boeing 737 planes to then procommunist Angola, the authorities at Boeing once agreed to pass on the following threatening message from an American agency to the ruling MPLA government of Angola:

> *"The MPLA would do well to heed our advice that no government can plan the reconstruction in post-war Angola without United States and Western help. No government can obtain the technical and financial resources to stimulate economic development without American consent. (. . .) The United States Government is prepared to think further about the supply of Boeing Aircraft to Angola and is willing to undertake further discussions depending on the courses of events in Angola."[92]*

Beyond the threat contained in that message, this is proof that someone in control of technology can use it as a means of obstructing someone else's progress in order to advance a desired cause. In this particular case, the United States is interested in removing the threat posed by communism. And it is trying to do so by letting Angola know

91   Lanning and Mueller, *Africa Undermined*, 229-256.

92   Robert J. Barnet, *The Lean Years: Politics in the Age of Scarcity* (New York: Simon and Schuster, 1980), 228.

that it is withholding technology from that country until that country mends its ways. But there's a bigger revelation in that threatening message: that America holds the key to Angola's economic development, which Angola cannot achieve without America's consent. I hasten to add that America will consent to development in Angola only if such development would not threaten America's interests. But since anything that makes Angola less dependent on America has the potential to threaten America's interests (and true development, by definition, has such a potential), we may conclude that America will not give its consent to the nurturing of such a potential threat. Therefore, America will not consent to development in Angola.

The very nature of international business makes it incompatible with the development process in the Third World. The need to safeguard their privileged position compels the foreign firms to control those factors to which they owe their privileges. What little technology or any other resources that trickle down to the poor countries in which they operate is due not to their benevolence but to the rivalry that often exists amongst them. The "invisible hand" is still governed, not by the entrepreneur's generosity but by his regard for his own interest. As Adam Smith put it, it is not from the benevolence of the butcher, the brewer, or the baker that we expect our dinner but from their regard for their own interests.

It follows from this that where it is less onerous to the butcher, the brewer, or the baker to preserve their interests without having to provide us with our dinner, they would abstain from making such provision. But since complete abstention cannot be envisaged, the tendency is for them to use ploys that allow them the chance of reducing the charge that the provision of our dinner brings on them. Business ethics may require that firms have as an objective the development of the countries in which they operate, but such an objective would certainly not be high on their list of priorities. For if it were so, their long-term interests would be in jeopardy.

To defend their unethical behavior in developing countries, foreign firms may argue (and rightly so) that if they discontinue their malpractices, they would jeopardize many jobs in their home countries and that the safeguarding of jobs at home is their primary ethical objective.[93] In these arguments, it is implied that there exists a conflict of interests between the foreign firm's home country and the one in which it invests. The firm then plays the central role of the arbiter. For obvious reasons, it will always be on the side of its home country. For one thing, its economic ties with the developing country can only be described as temporary. Jean-Baptiste Doumeng, the late French international business tycoon, came down in favor of his country when he declared to a group of pressmen that

> *"To me, what is important is to foster France's prestige. I will even go further: to create jobs for French citizens (. . .). I even recommend that we sell old and almost obsolete equipment so that our clients in the Third World will keep on placing new orders."[94] (MT)*

The author was merely voicing out what, undoubtedly, many in the North have been practicing over the years. His dishonesty he justified by arguing his case for France's prestige and for the need to provide jobs for his fellow citizens. What he failed to mention were the consequences of such practices on the economies of the importing countries, which, as he said, were the Third World.

As if to substantiate what his fellow Frenchman Jean-Baptiste Doumeng was just saying here above, Captain Paul Barril, an expert in counterterrorism operations in the special intervention unit of the National Gendarmerie (GIGN), in an interview published in the French version of *Playboy* magazine, told the story of how France sold old and obsolete equipment to Cameroon. He said,

---

93   Cees van Dam and Luud M. Stallaert, eds, *Trends in Business Ethics: Implications for Decision-Making,* vol. 3 (Leiden/Buston: Martinus Nijhoff Social Sciences Division, 1978), 2-3.

94   Quoted from an interview by Jean-Baptiste Doumeng in "Syndicat National de la Presse Privée et des Lettres d'information," reproduced by the French weekly *Le Canard Enchaîné.* (See article "Doumeng, alors" [Paris, March 17, 1982], 5.)

". . . Most of the time, [African] heads of State are ill-advised; sometimes [they are] deceived by French organisations whose sole aim is to sell them equipment which they don't need. (. . .) When the pope visited Cameroon, France made them buy automatic explosives detector robots. Each of them cost 2 million French Francs. One of them was used only twice and the tracks got broken. To replace one of those tracks costs 50.000 FF. The robots have been discarded and abandoned in one corner. They do not use them anymore. But what a big contract; and what huge sales commissions!"[95] *(MT)*

Effects of Integration

Efforts made to integrate further the Southern countries into the world economic system have ended up making the South more dependent on the North. This dependence is characterized by the following:

- Their concentration on the production of a narrow range of export products
- Their concentration on an equally narrow range of trading partners
- The high proportion of foreign trade relative to their GNPs
- The high level of debts services relative to their export earnings

The bargaining position of these countries has also been affected, with the result that

- they have become all the more reliant on allocated rather than self-generated growth,
- their ability to pursue desired policies is greatly reduced, and
- they are more exposed to pressure from multinationals, who may, therefore, press for protection, tax, and other concessions and expensive overhead capital investments that do not serve the interests of the host countries.

---

95   Christian Chatillon, "Capitaine Paul Barril," in French version of *Playboy* magazine (March 1995), 15.

As each Third World country specializes in the production and the export of only a narrow range of products, its resource mobility problems increase rather than decrease. In other words, the more specialized these countries become, the less mobile are their factors of production. And in that case, whatever comparative advantages enjoyed as a result specialization may be more than offset by the cost of their increased dependence. The Northern countries who constantly urge the Southern ones to specialize are not themselves specializing in the production of any given range of products. The tendency is for them to diversify as much as possible, even inventing synthetic substitutes for those products that traditionally came from the South. A good example is that of synthetic rubber products. These products are a testimony of the Northern countries' determination to diversify their activities and to defy natural pressures working in favor of international specialization. By subsidizing the growing of cotton in the North, they take that crop out of the hands of the South, which would otherwise enjoy a comparative advantage in its production and export.

Arrangements under which developed countries undertake to stabilize the earnings of primary exporters are, indeed, ploys used to prevent the Southern countries from diversifying. One such arrangement was the STABEX accord under which the EU countries provided funds to offset the effects of fluctuations in the output levels of certain primary products from their African, Caribbean, and Pacific partners. Curiously, that arrangement bore a strong resemblance to the prewar German foreign economic policies, which, as Albert O. Hirschman points out, were intended to prevent the industrialization of her agricultural trading partners.[96] In the same way, by providing stable incomes to agricultural export producers in the ACP countries, people there are encouraged to maintain, or even increase, their investment in agriculture, thereby neglecting investments in the manufacturing sector.

---

96   Albert O. Hirschman, *National Power and the Structure of Foreign Trade* (Berkeley: University of California Press, 1945), 36.

While at a bookstore recently, I came across a book whose telling title caught my attention. I did not buy the book, but I retained its title, which read *In Business as in Life, You Don't Get What You Deserve, You Get What You Negotiate*. Some trade negotiators from the North, intent on winning every available benefit for those they represent, seem to have learned that lesson only too well and are taking their job far too seriously. Unfortunately, as they press harder and harder to wring out every possible concession from their counterparts from the South, they end up making the exercise not worth the trouble for those from the South. As the negotiators from the North press for much more than their fair share of trade benefits that ought to accrue to both sides, those of the South see their own share of the same benefits dwindle and with it their interest in what is offered them. So they tend to resist further attempts to cheat them out of the benefits of trade, which only leads the negotiators from the North to be more aggressive, even bullish, in the quest for ever greater trade benefits for those they represent. Sometimes these negotiations go awry as was the case during trade talks between representatives of the European Union and those of some West African nations. Jean Ziegler tells the story:

> *"But when the West pretends to be negotiating with the people of the South, a time usually comes when the mask drops. That time came one fine day in Spring, 2007.*
> *In a large, sterile, windowless hall of the monstrous Varlimont building complex which houses the headquarters of the European Commission in Brussels, representatives of West Africa had been rejecting propositions (put forward) by European commissioners since early that morning.*
> *It was March 1st.*
> *Suddenly, the jovial Louis Michel, commissioner for development, lost all countenance. He threatened the Africans with economic reprisals, reminding them that the development funds could as*

*well be withheld at any moment. But to the great surprise of the
commissioners, the Africans did not take that lying down: they
caused the session to be adjourned.*

*Then the Nigerian ambassador convened a press conference in their
name. And it was the occasion for him to voice his anger at seeing the
Africans being treated like kids and like beggars. He also demanded
clarifications as to the future disbursements of the development aid
funds. He even dared to condemn the disgraceful tone used by certain
commissioners.*

*That same evening, Louis Michel publicly apologized to the African
representatives and regretted having allowed himself to be carried away.*

*. . . It is certain that the cynicism and the arrogance with which
Peter Mandelson, Louis Michel and Pascal Lammy try to break the
resistance of the people of the South contributes greatly to the rise in
the hatred of the West."[97] (MT)*

That, certainly, is not the only of such cases that have been
reported. In the book *Fair Trade for All*, the authors decry the unhealthy
atmosphere in which trade negotiations take place. They mention the
infamous Green Room process under which only a few chosen countries
from the developing world are invited to engage in direct talks with
the United States and the EU. They also recount the incident at the
Cancún conference of September 2003 when ministers from the Third
World refused to proceed with the agenda because they had come to the
conclusion that no agreement was better than a bad agreement. So they
scampered out of the conference center, and the chairman had to call off
the meeting.[98]

Another way of resisting development seems to be through the control
of population growth rates. If population growth is not controlled, it is
suspected that the world might become overpopulated sometime soon,

97   Jean Ziegler, *La haine de l'Occident* (Paris: Editions Albin Michel, 2008), 134-5.

98   Joseph E. Stiglitz and Andrew Charlton, *For Fair Trade For All: How Trade Can Promote
      Development* (Oxford: Oxford University Press, 2005), 63-4.

which will, in turn, increase the squeeze on available resources. Those countries whose per capita consumption of the said resources is presently amongst the highest have an interest in ensuring that these resources, which they have become accustomed to, and wherever they may be coming from, continue flowing to them. Were these resources to stop flowing, it would hurt their way of life. Unchecked population growth means that at some point in time, they are going to have to share the same limited supply of resources with many more people. In that case, unless other sources of supply are discovered or unless technology enables the production of suitable substitutes for these resources, things may not augur well for consumers of these resources. So it is reasonable to think that in those circumstances, those who stand to be hurt if the world population grows uncontrollably will find some way to influence it favorably.

The year 1974 saw the publication of a policy document called the *National Security Study Memorandum* (NSSM-200), or the Kissinger report, which explicitly laid out a detailed strategy by which the United States would aggressively promote population control in certain developing countries in order to make way for the United States to have unfettered access to the natural resources of these countries. According to this document, US foreign policy was to be designed and implemented in a manner to ensure a reduction in population growth in the designated countries (thirteen of them, including Nigeria, India, and Brazil). The NSSM-200 clearly acknowledged that the purpose of the policy was to serve the United States' strategic, economic, and military interests at the expense of developing countries. The NSSM-200 saw the growth in population in the developing world as a threat to US security in four basic ways, including its vital interest in strategic materials that have to be imported from the developing world.

Even though it was thought that some of the designated countries like Brazil and Nigeria would benefit politically and (maybe) economically from population growth, the document still recommended that their populations be curbed. This means that it was not with the developing countries' interests at heart that the policy was designed. It was to protect the interests of those whom the authors of the policy represent. Again, this goes to show that those in a privileged position will only naturally tend to defend their own interests when threatened, even when such defense might impede the progress of others.

Development in the South is also being resisted when the South is prevented from applying the very same trade policies that the developed countries once used. Today, trade liberalization is being touted as the only option open to the South if they hope to develop. But history tells us quite another story when it comes to the economic development of the North. The pattern was similar for most developed countries where the early stages of their development cycle were marked by policies intended to protect their infant industries. Britain, in the early stages of its Industrial Revolution, took all steps necessary to protect and promote its nascent industries. The Navigation Acts of 1707, for instance, were aimed at ensuring that all goods traded with Britain be transported on British ships, not on those of their rivals. Prime Minister Walpole's legislation of 1721 was intended to protect British manufacturing industries from foreign competition. The legislation provided for subsidies to encourage the export of British manufactured goods. It also called for the imposition of tariffs on foreign manufactured goods. Britain also tried to protect its manufacturing sector by discouraging it abroad, especially in some of its own colonies. For instance, it banned the import of cotton textile goods from India, which were said to be of superior quality to those of Britain. By passing the Wool Act of 1699, the British parliament also banned the trade in woollen cloths among British colonies, thus allowing only the woollen cloths of British manufacturers to be traded there. America too, even against the advice of Adam Smith, took steps to encourage its infant industry. In 1791, Alexander Hamilton, then US secretary of the treasury, presented a report to Congress in which he recommended the protecting of the country's industries from foreign competition.

Such protectionist policies generally remained in place until such time that the home industries were deemed strong and efficient enough to compete favorably with foreign manufacturers and that, for it to continue to grow, it was now in the country's interest to find a liberalized market.

The truth of the matter is that every economy, at some stage (usually, early in its evolutionary cycle), needs some breathing space in which it can take its first faltering steps. A protected economy provides such a breathing space. Calling for the lifting of such protection in the South, whose economies are only just attempting to start developing, is tantamount to resisting development there.

People . . . must be able to control their own activities within the framework of their . . . communities. At present, the best intentioned governments—my own included—too readily move from a conviction of the need for rural development into acting as if people had no ideas of their own. This is quite wrong . . . people do know what their basic needs are . . . if they have sufficient freedom, they can be relied upon to determine their priorities for development.
—President J. K. Nyerere

The poor of the world cannot be helped by mass production, only by production by the masses.
—Mahatma Gandhi

Between nations, there is no such thing as generosity. If anything, there is intelligent egoism.
—Anonymous

CHAPTER V

Conclusion and Comments

In the preceding chapters, I have tried to give a brief description of the international setting in which development in the poor countries is taking place. It is clear, from what was discussed, that the international economic environment is constantly changing. Changes that have taken place in the last two centuries have been militant both for and against development in the South. Of course, our reservoir of technical and scientific knowledge is fuller today than it was before the Industrial Revolution in England. But the near-exclusive control of the pool of knowledge by the ones constitutes a tremendous obstacle to the development of the others inasmuch as those in control are reluctant to diffuse it.

In our greatly changed environment, it is hardly likely that some of the recipes that were instrumental in the transformation of the now-developed countries would produce similar effects when applied to the problems confronting today's developing countries. Nor are many of those recipes still available to them. For one thing, some of them have been taken off the table. As if in a bid to kick away the ladder that the developed countries once used to climb out of underdevelopment, these same developed countries are now dissuading the developing countries from imitating them. Some people in the developed countries now consider that it would be inappropriate for developing countries to become like the United States or Western European countries.

But there are other reasons why development may not be feasible for the rest of the world. The need to fight wars compelled England to develop powerful arms and shipbuilding industries. Knowledge and experience gained in the process were later applied to other branches of the economic activity. Almost all wars in the past quarter century have been fought in developing countries. Yet there has been no such compulsion on people of these areas to invest in the arms industry. The reason for this being that their war requirements have readily been met by suppliers in developed countries. And not only do these wars cause physical damage in developing countries, but the economies of these warring countries do not even benefit from the spin-offs inherent in arms development and production.

International trade was instrumental in the economic expansion of England and other developed countries. Their trade with the rest of the world was done on largely favorable terms, which enabled them to enrich themselves at the expense of the others. It is known that in many cases, England was able to dictate prices both for the goods she imported as well as for the ones she exported. Her colonies constituted large captive markets for both finished goods and primary products. Today, there exist no new colonies to which developing countries can expect to export the products of their industries.[99] Markets in the North are already saturated with the types of manufactured goods developing countries are capable of exporting.

It was also known that at the time of the Industrial Revolution in England, capital outlay for industry was small. So too were interest rates. Technology was relatively simple. Market prospects were goods, so even the least ambitious entrepreneurs were willing to invest. Whenever the need arose, the government of England was willing to and capable

---

99   Even if such new colonies existed, it would be unlikely that the South be allowed priority of access to their markets. The attitude of some Northern states regarding the question of the extraction and the sharing out of the resources of the seabeds of international waters suggests that they are as unwilling as ever to make any concessions.

of discouraging industry abroad in order to ensure markets for her manufactures. Her entrepreneurs were thus relieved of the constraints of protectionism by foreign countries.

These favorable conditions do not exist today for developing countries. Trade terms are very unfavorable to them. Markets in the North are protected against finished goods from the South. Capital layouts, even for small ventures, are generally higher now than they were two centuries ago. Given the narrowness of home markets, industry in the South is unable to benefit from economies of scale.

The North's control over communication media enables them to influence consumption habits in the South, which explains why in the developing countries certain goods imported from the North are preferred to their locally produced equivalents.

Experience has often shown that similar economic policies applied to different situations do not always achieve the same degree of success. In the early 1980s, the newly elected Mitterrand government of France tried to revive the French economy by adopting Keynesian policies. It did not work. Yet similar policies were the driving forces behind the recovery of the American and, indeed, the world economy of the '30s.

The changed economic environment aside, it can be said (from what we have shown here so far) that the continued state of underdevelopment in the Southern countries is, at least in part, due to resistance to progress. While it is possible to transfer economic factors around the globe today, thanks to globalization, it is still very hard to resist the urges of self-interest. As it has been shown here, this resistance stems from the Northern countries' desire to preserve their privileges. The insufficiency of capital in the South can, therefore, be seen as resulting from a process of uneven distribution of resources in which more resources leave the poor countries than enter therein. France's president François Mitterrand was making just this point in his *Discours de la Baulle* when he said, "When I realize that the flow of capital from the poor South to the rich

North is greater than the flow of capital from the rich North to the poor South, I know that something is wrong."

There is, therefore, a need for a new development strategy—a strategy based on the new equation in which the changing world setting and the natural inclination to resist development are given full consideration. It is necessary, for the formulation of such a strategy, to dispense with the long-held view that development aid can be granted free of charge. The new strategy must recognize the fact that the world economic setting still has the traits of a jungle. It is a jungle in which each nation struggles against all other nations—one in which the need to defend common interests may force some countries to enter into alliances. But such alliances do not in any way imply the removal of all other conflicts that exist between them. It is a jungle in which every nation's or every group of nations' strategy is determined by the need to protect their own interests. It would, therefore, be naïve to expect benevolent assistance from those against whom a nation or a group of nations is supposedly struggling.

The availability of excess quantities of goods and services is no guarantee that they will be equitably distributed. There exist large quantities of excess farm produce in Western Europe and North America today. Yet even in those same countries, some people sometimes go hungry. There exists enough food in the world to feed every mouth, yet some, especially in the Third World, go hungry. The paradox is easy to explain. The artificial distinction made between production and functional distribution overlooks the important fact that in a great majority of cases, only those who take part (directly or indirectly) in the production process are entitled to compensation in the form of wages, interests, rents, or profits. To most people, participation in the production process involves the selling or the hiring out of their labor. For most people, labor is the only commodity, the only resource that they have to offer as contribution to the production process. Where they are unable to sell such labor, they automatically lose their right to all material compensation. This is true for all other classes of income earners, the stockholders, as well as the entrepreneurs. If you deprive landowners of a chance to rent out their property or to invest in a productive venture, you deprive them of a chance to share in the revenue generated by such a venture. Technical innovations may increase the economy's productive capacities well beyond those required to satisfy every need, but those whose resources were not engaged in the production would still be deprived of a part of the output. And if such innovations resulted in the displacement of some labor, the owners of such labor would lose their claim to a share of the output. The reason for this being that such increased productive capacities occurred without their being able to sell their labor or rent out the capital, which they hold.[100]

Considering the global economy as a whole, it can be stated that its output capacity for certain goods exceeds its needs. The countries of the North account for a very great part of the world output of goods and services, hence the very large share of the "cake" that they get. Deprived of a chance to employ their own factors of production—especially labor and local raw materials—in a world saddled with excess productive capacities, the Southern countries cannot expect to get a share of the world output of goods and services that is commensurate with their needs. By contrast, the advanced countries, who manage to employ a greater part of their stock of productive resources in the production process, can take pleasure in stockpiling or hoarding goods and services that they may never get around to consuming.

One is tempted to think that there exists a correlation between the use of one's factors of production and the right to a reasonable share of the output. Yes, there is. For as was observed earlier on, only those whose factors of production contribute to the input are entitled to a share of the output. And the share of the output to which they have right is commensurate not with their needs but with their input. This leads, naturally, to the conclusion that every society—as, indeed, every able-bodied person within it—ought

100   In developed societies, the jobless are entitled to unemployment allowance either on the understanding that they contribute to the unemployment fund when they eventually get employed or because they had done so when they were working.

to have a chance to use, sell, or employ their resources in a productive manner. Such a conclusion may have far-reaching implications. For it means that in a long run, all countries should be self-sufficient, allowing, however, for the necessities of international trade (caused by the uneven endowment of natural resources over the globe). It also means that the quantities of goods and services (over and above those that are required for home consumption) that a country produces shall be equal in value to the quantity of goods and services it needs to import. That would result in a trade balance for each country. The aim of such a policy is not to impose autarchy but rather to ensure the development and use of each country's own economic potentials for its own good.

Anything near a fair distribution of income can be achieved only if there is a fair sharing of employment opportunities for all factors of production.

Development Strategies

Whatever the development strategy that a society adopts, consideration must be given to the consequences that change is likely to produce. The ruling class and the elite in developing countries will accept only a development that does not threaten their positions. Unfortunately, the powerful positions they occupy make their consent a precondition for development.

Unlike in Europe where the capitalist class replaced feudal power, capitalist development in the Third World is only strengthening the powers of the ruling class.[101] The privileged positions that the elite of developing countries occupy (and that they naturally tend to defend) usually expose them to acts of bribery, corruption, and patronage. And the exercise of patronage enables them to maintain these privileged positions. But such positions lack a strong basis. Although enjoying the support of the capitalist class (to which patronage is distributed), the

---

101   I am indebted to Michael Lipton for this point that he develops in his book *Why Poor People Stay Poor* (Cambridge, Massachusetts: Harvard University Press, 1977), 39.

ruling class cannot enjoy real power. For power to be real, it must be grounded on a strong economy. The ruling class in the Third World is thus exposed to coercion from the Northern interests groups acting either directly or through the local bourgeois class. Such power, based on direct or indirect external support, will always be vulnerable.

A characteristic of Third World capitalism is that it is chiefly concerned with the distribution rather than the production of goods. Gains from commerce are either plowed back into the profession or spent on imported luxury goods. Relatively little is invested in the manufacturing sectors, with the result that very little, if any, is gained through the learning process. Another important result of this trader capitalism is the strengthening of economic ties with the Northern countries, which supply most of the manufactured goods distributed in the South and which also represent the essential markets for primary products.

What is often forgotten is that the enhancement of the power of government depends upon the latter's responsiveness to the aspirations of its people—not just those of the capitalist class. Governments of developing countries can enhance their power and self-assurance by being responsive to the aspirations of their peoples. These aspirations include the craving for advancement: education and training that lead to employment, infrastructure facilities, etc. Satisfying this desire for advancement requires that there exists, among other things, an indigenous industrial capitalist class—not just the commercial one— to champion the struggle for economic development. In conflicts that are likely to erupt between local industrialists and representatives of foreign interests, a Third World government should be able to take sides with the former. The laws it enacts must reflect its desire to protect the emergent industrial sector. (But such protection must not be at the expense of either the industrial working class or the consumers.)

A small dose of paternalism will not necessarily be harmful to a developing economy. The ASEAN governments are very active in promoting economic development in those countries. This they do by investing directly in the economy or by awarding public contracts to indigenous firms. The guiding hand of the Japanese government was described by E. Herbert Norman when he wrote,

> *"Japan skipped from feudalism into capitalism omitting the laissez-faire stage and its political counterpart, Victorian liberalism . . . (Her leaders) were so far in advance of the rest of their countrymen that they had to drag a complaining, half-awakened nation of merchants and peasant after them. The autocratic or paternalistic way seemed to the Meji leaders the only possible method if Japan was not to sink into the ranks of a colonial country.*"[102]

It is the duty of the government to create the right and enabling environment in which local industrial capitalism can take root, grow, and flourish. It is with the aid of a strong national or regional economy, owned and managed by the indigenous business community, that a Third World country can expect to put up resistance to economic and political coercions from abroad. All durable power must be grounded on a solid economy. A disciplined, strong local business class is necessary—though not sufficient—for establishing such a solid economy. And it is up to the state to encourage the creation of such a community. Government support and protection are needed to resist the assault of foreign companies and to facilitate capital formation. Even the newly developed countries of Southeast Asia had recourse to such practices in the past. It was seen earlier on that England protected her industry both at home and abroad. Not only did she prohibit the import of certain goods but also went as far as to destroy industry in other countries. Local banks should be encouraged to grant greater credit facilities to indigenous entrepreneurs than to foreign investors. For example, foreign firms may be allowed to borrow only up to 10 or 20 percent of their capital requirements

---

102   E. Herbert Norman, *Japan's Emergence as a Modern State* (New York: Institute of Pacific Relations, 1946), 47.

from the local financial markets whereas the indigenous firms should be allowed to borrow as much as 40 or 50 percent. Even greater credit facilities need to be given to those investing in the industry.

It was observed earlier on that investments by the Northern countries in the Third World tend to increase the dependence of the latter either by being capital-intensive (with capital goods imported from the North) or by producing for vertically integrated markets. It was also observed that, in either case, the host country was placed in a position in which it was impossible to act against the interests of the Northern countries without creating discontent among the local populations. From the Northern countries' point of view, the capital requirements of developing nations are a problem insoluble without their (the Northern countries') aid. Export production is thus presented as the only means of meeting these requirements. But as we have already observed, this argument also serves as a pretext for the implementation of policies designed to make the escape from domination difficult.

To check the adverse effects of such an investment pattern, policies in developing countries require only that

- priority be given to production for domestic markets and
- labor-intensive projects be given precedence over capital-intensive ones as this will create the opportunity for hiring local labor.

The domestic-market-cum-labor-intensive strategy has two important advantages:

- The country can exert greater control over their home markets than they can over foreign ones.[103]
- The problem of capital shortage would be greatly reduced as certain machines are replaced by labor.

---

103   A regional market can be assimilated to a domestic one if goods and services are allowed to circulate freely among member countries and if concerted actions can be taken against products from outside the region.

Although studies show that labor-abundant countries would create more jobs if they adopted an outward-looking rather than an inward-looking industrial strategy, the expected gains from the economies of large scale would be obtained only if their products found markets.[104] Given the protective tendencies of trade policies in the developed world, there is very little evidence to suggest that such markets exist or will exist in the future. Foreign markets, where they do exist, are likely to get saturated or protected by those governments who adopt protective policies as a means of preserving jobs at home. Trying to resolve the problem of unemployment by adopting an outward-looking strategy may turn out to be a wild-goose chase. The pursuit of an outward-looking industrial strategy would be beneficial only if there were guarantees that exports would not be restricted by trade barriers. Such guarantees are easily obtainable only within the framework of regional groupings involving a number of developing countries. Within such a framework, member countries can take concerted actions against goods coming from outside the region. In the absence of such a regional understanding, the inward-looking strategy seems the better option bargain.

But this strategy brings to the forefront another important question—that of adapting the size of industry to the small internal market. This question will be considered in a later section.

International Trade

The risk run by developing countries as a consequence of their overinvolvement in international trade has already been pointed out. Any reasonable policy in this domain must aim at reducing their dependence on trade with the North. As has already been observed, there is no point in trying to persuade the North to change its mind and trade with the South on more equitable terms. Such would be an irrational decision

104   J. Sheahan, *Trade and Employment: Industrial Exports Compared to Import Substitution in Mexico* (Williamstown, Massachusetts: Williams College Centre for Development Economics, Research Memorandum 43, 1971). See also L. E. Westphal and K. S. Kim, *Industrial Policy and Development in Korea* (mimeo., Washington: Development Research Centre, International Bank for Reconstruction and Development, 1973).

on its part. Any real improvements in trade terms will not result from negotiations. They will result only from improvements in the bargaining position of the South. As long as the economies of the LDCs remain vulnerable, as long as they remain heavily dependent on trade with the North, it is hard to see how the latter would be willing to pay more for what it knows it can obtain at a cheaper price. Nor will it, under these circumstances, refrain from making attractive commercial profits when it knows it can easily dictate prices for those goods for which the LDCs remains a captive market. The events that led to the oil crisis in the '70s have shown that changes in trade terms do not always result from negotiations between exporters and importers of a commodity. The petroleum-exporting countries did not have to negotiate price increases with the importing ones. They just raised it.

It was also argued that foreign trade (especially that based on international specialization) was not always beneficial to a developing country. At best, the Southern countries do not benefit as much from trading with the Northern ones as they ought to. At worst, they are worse off than they would be if a great deal less of their trade were conducted with the Northern countries.

There is, therefore, a need for trade diversification in the South. Two forms of diversification are needed here. The first would aim at widening the range of their trading partners amongst fellow developing nations, and the second would seek to expand their export-product mix.

Two other simultaneous movements are necessary: a gradual economic disengagement from the North and increased regional integration.[105] It is in the interest of developing countries to create or strengthen regional economic groupings. By so creating larger markets, their industries would benefit from the economies of large scale, which, in turn, would help bring down the unit price of goods they produce and market. Within the framework of such regional markets, they would be able to take effective protective measures in favor of their own infant industries.

---

105   For very obvious reasons, total economic disengagement is neither desirable nor feasible.

It is, however, to be noted that regional groupings, inasmuch as they call for joint economic planning, are problematic. We must not underestimate the problems likely to be encountered when drawing up a development plan acceptable to all member countries of a regional market. Experience has shown that, for reasons of prestige, every developing country wants to have its own gas or petroleum industry or its own steel complex. The proliferation of a certain kind of industry in Africa is due in part to the lack of a region investment plan to avoid investing in the same type of industries, which may result in their factories operating at well below full capacity. After the Central African countries of Cameroon, Congo, and Gabon individually invested in sugar production, they ended up with excess capacities on their hands. Had they concerted their investment decisions, knowing that they belonged to the same trading region and so could export their product across their borders, they would have avoided much of the wasteful investment altogether.

**Table showing production levels in sugar refineries
in three Central African Countries**

Country	N° of Factories	Output Capacity (tons p.a.)	Actual production level	% of prod. Level over capacity
Congo	2	135.000	5.700	0.04
Gabon	1	30.000	9.300	0.31
Cameroon	2	80.000	44.200	0.55

Source: Bulletin de l'Afrique Noire. N° 1070, Paris, 26th Nov. 1980

Regional economic planning may help avoid the setting up of industries that turn out to be wastefully competitive rather than profitably complementary. By agreeing on a common industrial plan, a group of countries may be able to use their acquired productive capacities more efficiently.

The creation of a viable regional market depends both on political will and on economic capacity. Reluctance on the part of politicians to engage in regional planning stems from their fear of losing what is left of their national sovereignties. But developing countries will have to weigh the prospects of gains from economic regionalization against unproductive national economies.

Capital Formation

It is yet to be shown that the economies of the poor countries are not capable of generating profits. If this were so, foreign investors would have no reason to invest in these countries. That they should continue to invest in the Third World despite the risk of political instability is proof of the possibility of profit generation. The volume of capital generated in the South is much greater than most authors are willing to admit. The problem facing most Third World countries is rather that of gaining and retaining the generated capital within their economies. Given the prevalent climate of political instability in these countries, foreign investors who still dare to invest there are anxious to repatriate their earnings as soon as they are realized, which makes capital formation difficult. Political instability increases the risk of loss, which, in turn, increases the cost of capital and decreases profit margins. And as profit margins drop, the capacity for capital formation reduces. Those to whom profits accrue, who are often the ones in a position to effect capital formation, may not see the need to carry out further profitable investments in the country. So they tend to use their earnings in ways that are not productive or to make investments in other countries where there is greater stability. The usual strategy of the MNCs who invest in the Third World is to choose the shortest payback periods possible for their investments. The huge cash flows so generated are then repatriated to safer havens, thus interfering with the process of capital accumulation in the host country.

Although the fear of the risk of political instability is often cited as the reason for such a practice, another reason could be that since foreign investment can enhance greater efficiency in the local business community, there would be fewer openings for the demonstration of superior foreign techniques of management skills and know-how. And since efficiency comes with time, it is reasonable to suppose that the longer the local capitalist class is exposed to foreign expertise and techniques, the more it is likely to learn. And the more it becomes efficient, the more active will be its challenge to the foreign investors. In that case, the foreign investor's return on investments (ROI) will tend to diminish with increasing competition and time.[106]

A further proof that capital shortage is not so acute in the South is that only a very small fraction of capital investments in these countries comes from abroad. Foreign investors generally generate much of their capital requirements locally. Studies made by C. F. Bergsten, T. Horst, and T. H. Moran[107] showed that only between 20 and 25 percent of the funds invested annually by American multinationals in developing countries comes from the United States. The remainder is borrowed in the local financial markets or transferred from other countries.

Table showing sources of funds used by American firms
in the LDCs, 1966-72

Year	Retained earnings	Depreciation	Others	US funds	Debts from Affiliates	From foreign sources	Foreign equity
1966	25	25	-2	20	4	26	2
1967	12	32	-5	25	2	29	4
1968	18	21	1	8	2	29	4
1969	15	24	n.a.	31	1	27	3
1970	7	33	3	13	7	36	2
1971	13	40	9	21	-4	24	-4
1972	13	22	n.a.	24	2	37	-2

Source: From authors' Estimates based on data published by Survey of Current Business: (vol. 55, July 1975, p. 31).

---

106   Once again, this reveals the existence of conflicts between the long- and short-run consequences of foreign investments in the LDCs.

107   C. F. Bergsten, T. Horst, and T. H. Moran, *American Multinationals and American Interest* (Washington, DC: Brookings Institution, 1978).

The authors of the study suggested that MNCs enjoy preferential treatment from financial institutions in the host countries.[108] That explained why they might have been able to capture the best investment opportunities to the detriment of the local capital class.

In the face of such overwhelming advantages, the local business community may not respond with adequate vigor but rather deteriorate and liquidate. Joseph Stiglitz, in his book, *Globalization and Its Discontents*, says that

> *'When global financial institutions enter a country, they can squelch the domestic competition. And as they attract depositors away from the local banks in a country like Ethiopia, they may be far more attentive and generous when making loans to large multinational corporations than they will to providing credit to small businesses and farmers.'[109]*

The inability of the African entrepreneur to raise capital has sometimes been blamed on that continent's system of *economy of affection*, which Göran Hydén defines as one which

> *". . . denotes a network of support, communications and interaction among structurally defined groups connected by blood, kin, community or other affinities, for example, religion. It links together in a systematic fashion a variety of discrete economic and social units which in other regards may be autonomous . . ."[110]*

In short, Hydén's *economy of affection* concerns groups that others call extended families. The economy of affection probably constitutes an obstacle to capital accumulation. But as the author says, it serves

---

108   Ibid., 361.

109   Joseph Stiglitz, *Globalization and Its Discontents*, 31.

110   Göran Hydén, *No Shortcuts to Progress: African Development Management in Perspective* (London: Heinemann, 1983), 8.

some very important functional purposes, which he places under three headings:

(a) basic survival, (b) social maintenance, and (c) development.[111] However, the economy of affection may not be entirely

unproductive. If the well-to-do, in an effort to raise capital, failed to fulfill their obligations toward their extended families, the society in general would have to do it in their place. In which case, the society would have to draw on the resources of the rich (by way of taxes) to cover the cost of education, health, and other social services offered to the children of the poor. This, as can be expected, would equally militate against capital formation. If, like the rich members of society, the government decides against the provision of these services to the poor, there would emerge few educated, healthy, and thus, employable people on the one hand and a multitude of unqualified and, therefore, unemployable people on the other. In either case, society will not be anywhere nearer its development objectives, for there will be a gross imbalance in its resource mix: a surplus of capital goods over human capital. The economy of affection, therefore, contributes directly in the struggle for development by assisting in establishing one of its prerequisites, namely, the formation of an employable labor force.

The volume of capital requirement depends on several factors, two of which are the type of technology involved and the size of the investment. In the face of capital shortage, it would be reasonable that developing countries choose those production methods for which capital inputs are small. So a maximum of those factors of production they have in abundance (labor and land) could be employed. The tendency for developing countries to import the newest equipment and the latest production techniques and their liking for prestige projects militates against capital sufficiency. A more rational attitude would be to import cheap equipment incorporating appropriate technology. Care has to be taken to ensure that spare parts for all the imported equipment will be

---

111   Ibid., 11.

available throughout their lifetime. In the absence of such a guaranty, the importing countries may be transformed into a graveyard of obsolete equipment from the North.

Agriculture and Migration

Migration has been suggested as a means of combating mass poverty and underdevelopment. However, it will be acceptable as a solution to these problems only in certain cases.[112]

War or drought may force people to leave their homeland. Migration may also be the only option where there is a shortage of arable land or where employment opportunities do not exist. Even here, migration may be only the lesser evil. For one thing, the most ambitious and the most apt to effect change are usually the ones who are most able to migrate.

Not all migration is beneficial to an economy. Take, for instance, the case of young Sudanese who, at the completion of their technical education, migrate to Saudi Arabia or Kuwait where they expect to find jobs with much higher pay than what obtains in their country. Their departure represents a great loss to the Sudanese economy. The same is true for the departure of all other personnel who leave their countries to work abroad.

Emigration will be beneficial to society only if

- it is temporary and
- while away, the emigrants are given the occasion to acquire knowledge and/or other resources that are in short supply in their homes.

In the absence of these conditions, emigration may not prove beneficial to the home countries of the emigrants. The millions of Egyptians working in the Gulf countries are sending back to their villages an estimated six billion to ten billion dollars annually.[113] It is estimated the Cameroonians living abroad send home or remit home

---

112   J. K. Galbraith, *The Nature of Mass Poverty* (England: Penguin Books, 1980).

113   *International Herald Tribune* (Paris, February 1, 1985), 5.

annually more than three hundred million dollars. Needless to say that demand and investments there would be stimulated as a result of the inflow of money. In the same way, Europe's immigrant workers will help stimulate economic activities in their home countries if they are allowed to repatriate a substantial part of their earnings. Their home economies will gain even more as a result of their emigration if while abroad, they acquire knowledge or skills that will be useful to them at home—knowledge and skills they would not have acquired if they did not immigrate.

Exposure to life in a developed society will instill in the immigrant the desire to seek improvements in his or her own society. Returning immigrant workers would almost certainly seek to practice the trade they learned while abroad or go into business. Even those who, because of lack of financial resources, were not able to further their education at home might have a chance to do so once in a foreign land.

Many students from Third World countries studying in Western Europe and North America finance their own education with their earnings from the menial jobs they do—jobs they would certainly not accept to do in their home countries. Therefore, restricting the emigration of those who presently are unable to make contributions to the economy (but who, if allowed to go abroad, would return home enriched intellectually or materially) may, indeed, be obstructing rather than promoting development. Their stay abroad might make them more apt to make substantial contributions to the economic life of their country.

However, there are chances that some of those who emigrate as a means of escaping from mass poverty will remain abroad. But there are even greater chances that many of those who went away poor and only partially educated will return home more educated or richer or both.

The more common type of migration takes place within the same country. People simply move from their villages to the big towns and cities. The main cause of this kind of migration seems to be the impossibility of finding employment in the rural areas. Often, it is only in the big commercial centers that there is hope of finding employment. Another cause could be the difference in the standard of living between the towns and the villages. A poor country's few social amenities are usually available only in the towns. Medical, educational, and administrative services are available only in the towns.

However, the standard of living in those overcrowded shantytowns on the outskirts of cities like Lagos or Douala is not much higher than it is in the villages from which the migrants came.

In Latin America, recent waves of migration are due to the inability of peasants to gain access to land (a few landlords control most of the arable land). Added to that, the drought in the northeast of Brazil forced many people to move southward to the industrial centers.

Policies aimed at checking migration must, therefore, provide solutions to the different problems just mentioned above. Most people would probably opt for life in small towns and villages if they were sure to find gainful employment and the very basic social amenities there. A reasonable strategy would require that the people themselves be associated with projects aimed at providing these amenities. It should start first with the process of identifying their priorities. Most community development projects in the Third World do not succeed because they are introduced from without. The needs of the people for whom the projects are intended are not given full consideration.

The construction of a health-care center, a postal agency, a school, etc., in the rural area can be borne partly by the central or the local government and partly by the people of the area. While the government undertakes to provide those materials and know-how that cannot be obtained locally, the people could be counted upon to contribute the rest, including the labor needed to carry out construction work. In certain rural areas of Cameroon where pipe-borne water was once available, the rural people were instrumental in choosing as well as in carrying out the projects. This was, for instance, the case with villages like Kembong and Ossing in Manyu Division in Cameroon. In both cases, apart from money contributions, the villagers participated in the various phases of construction work. It must be stated, however, that both villages received assistance from the government as well as from certain foreign-aid organizations. But the fact remains that without the people's direct involvement, those projects would not have been successfully executed at the time.

Such self-help projects have a very important advantage: they promote the learning process. Some of those who participate in the construction work are likely to end up as bricklayers, plumbers, electricians, or carpenters. Some of them may also pick up management skills.

Since most governments of Third World countries are unable to provide such basic needs as water, medical care, and education to people in the rural area, it is for them (the governments) to encourage these people to provide for themselves. The type of campaign that characterized the Green Revolution in certain African countries could also be launched to incite people to continue to improve their own living conditions. Government-controlled news agencies could take the lead in such a campaign. Where need be, financial incentives such as tax cuts could be granted to communities who undertake self-projects.

Medical expenditure should reflect government desire to encourage people to train in preventive medicine. As it is often said, prevention is better than cure. The trained personnel would then go into the countryside to advise the people on their health problems. Small, village-sized health units are better adapted to the practice of preventive medicine than the sophisticated or specialized hospitals. Clearly, the latter would absorb large amounts of valuable foreign exchange, and their services would be available only to people in the cities. Not that people from the rural areas are barred from seeking medical care in hospitals, but the problems involved in getting such care are big enough to deter them from going there for help. For instance, the farther away from the hospital, the more it costs to travel there, and so the more reluctant will be the sick to go there for treatment. An even greater deterrent is the inadequacy of services provided in most hospitals. Hospitalized patients have to provide their own food, do their laundry themselves, and go out to the pharmacy for drugs. This means that those who get admitted into the hospital have to be accompanied by someone from their home to provide these services. This also raises the question of lodging for those accompanying the patients. Accommodation is usually provided only to the patients and not to their attendants.

To retain the population in the rural areas, it certainly would not do to provide them with only basic amenities. The temptation to migrate to big towns will be successfully resisted only if there exists in the villages the possibility of obtaining gainful employment there.

Encouragement needs to be given to those who wish to set up as artisans or small entrepreneurs. Investing in the rural area could prove economically viable if small and simple production machinery were used. Soap—or *garri*-making units could be successfully run by the people with only very little knowledge of science and management.

Small-scale investments present several advantages: the break-even point is generally very low, with the result that even at a very low output level, profit can still be made. Small industries also tend to use local raw materials, labor, as well as energy resources. They create demand for small-scale capital goods that an emergent, indigenous capital-goods sector may be able to satisfy without much difficulty. The same capital-goods sector should be able to manufacture improved but simple machinery for the agricultural sector.

Given the proximity of the market to the points of production, there should arise no major distribution problems, at least not during the early stages of the venture.

Perhaps, Third World countries need to learn from the Indians. There exist, in most parts of India, government agencies whose function is to recruit and train would-be self-employed people in rural areas. Under their Entrepreneurial Development Program, respondents are screened on the basis of their risk-taking abilities, need for achievement, sense of efficacy, past experience, knowledge, skills, aptitude to start up a business, etc. They are given a short course on the social and psychological aspects of entrepreneurship and the management of a new enterprise. This is followed by practical fieldwork for a length of time. Successful candidates are then given both financial and technical assistance to start up their own business in rural areas.[114]

Local research institutions could play a very important role in the gathering, the developing, and the diffusing of information on improved production methods. The Kumasi University Consultancy Centre was instrumental in the adoption of simple production processes by all investors in Ghana. The best known of its successes is the soap-making process. It was a process that became generally accepted among the rural population of Ghana and was beginning to gain acceptance in other countries such as Mali, where it was implanted a few years later.[115] Similar institutions exist already in many developing countries, but their activities as well as their products are still totally unknown to the public. The local business community cannot be expected to try out new processes without information relative to them.

A sector greatly affected by rural/urban migration is agriculture. Output, except for certain export crops, is constantly falling in most developing countries, with the result that they become increasingly dependent on imported food for the local populations. In the absence of any substantial increase in productivity, the reduction in the number of farmworkers due to this exodus has resulted in a fall in total agricultural output. Peasants are generally encouraged to increase their production of export crops. The market assurance given for this category of farm

---

114   These programs are open only to people who have already learned a trade but who lack the financial resources and/or sufficient motivation to start up their own business. For further reading, see paper by P. D. Malgavkar, "The Role of Techno-Entrepreneurs in the Adoption to New Technology" in *Appropriate Technology: Problem and Promises*, ed. Nicolas Jéquier (Paris: OECD Development Centre Studies, 1976), 189-205.

115   Derek Miles, "Développement, Transfert et Diffusion de la Technologie," *Le Courrier: ACP-Communauté Européenne* (Brussels: Bimestriel no. 83, Jan-Fev. 1984), 67-8.

produce is an important incentive that is absent in the case of markets for local food crops. In many cases, there is no organized system of distribution for locally consumed produce. So even where both supply and demand exist, they are unlikely to obtain satisfaction.

Increases in food production can be achieved either by the employment of more people on the land or by the improvement of farming methods. In either case, those who accept to remain on the land need great encouragement. The departure of people from the lands and the consequent fall in agricultural output are primarily due to the lack of incentives. This runs against the generally held view that lack of improved techniques of farming is the main obstacle to increased agricultural output. A lot may be done by way of training facilities. But as long as agricultural labor is considered unattractive, these efforts will not attain the desired objectives. In practice, farming, like many other technical professions, is considered a trade for all those who have not succeeded in other fields. This is why, despite the occupational opportunities that vocational or agricultural training offers, many young people prefer an academic career. The oversaturation of the market for clerical job seekers has not succeeded in deterring would-be white-collar job seekers. Access to most highly paid jobs is still achieved through academic-style education, which, therefore, remains more attractive to most people of school age. The artisan, the technician, and especially, the farmer are thought of as playing inferior roles in society. The financial rewards are, on the average, lower than those that can be obtained by people with an academic-style education.

Even where some form of vocational training is available, some of those who opt for it do so against their will. Experience has shown that many of them accept to undertake vocational training only with the view to using it as a stepping stone. Many of those who receive vocational training do, at one time or another, seek to break away and join the mainstream constituted by academicians despite the growing scarcity of job opportunities for the latter. The average artisan or technician has no chance of climbing to a top position in his profession, so his status remains the same over the years.

It takes more than just vocational agricultural instructions to induce people, especially the young, to take up farming activities. Incentives to those entering agricultural or technical professions must come primarily in the form of increased financial rewards. There need to be set up market structures through which food can be channeled from areas with a surplus output to those where harvest is poor. The governments of developing countries should provide social overhead capital: farm-to-market roads, transport and storage facilities, etc. They should encourage the setting up of agricultural cooperative societies in which farmers would actively take part. Credit facilities should involve a low interest rate and be spread over sufficiently long periods. Frequent refresher courses should be organized for practicing agricultural workers. It is they who are most likely to remain on the land after their training.

Simultaneously, the governments of Third World countries must encourage research in agricultural production in conjunction with educational institutions. Emphasis must be laid on the development and manufacture of more productive farm implements. Research should also be carried out on food conservation methods. This is a particularly important point that must not be neglected if farmers are to be encouraged to produce food in quantities greater than those they can reasonably expect to consume or sell within a short period of time. One reason why these farmers choose to produce for the export market is the fear of not finding enough buyers of local foodstuff before it goes bad. Good, low-cost preservation methods will increase considerably the length of time during which they can expect to find markets for their produce. This will incite the production of more food for domestic use than is generally required for short-term purposes. This could be done in collaboration with the agro-industrial sector, which would constitute a major market for farm produce.

Appropriate Technology

For the Third World countries to augment their productive capacities, for them to be able to use their resources more efficiently, there needs to be an improvement in their methods of production. There is a need for new technology. They need technology that would neither increase their dependence on developed countries nor escape their mastery. It is only under such conditions that acquired knowledge can contribute to their economic development. Besides the danger of dependence, the habit of importing technology is also quite incompatible with the learning process through which a country can expect to develop its own production procedures. The need for other sources of technical and scientific knowledge is, therefore, evident. At present, very little is being done by way of research and development in the Third World. R&D are no doubt costly, time consuming, and painstaking. And what is more, the results are usually unpredictable. But despite the high degree of uncertainty involved, the effects of R&D on the learning process are usually beneficial. They provide, perhaps, the only real guaranty that a country can have against exploitation based on the scarcity of technology.

No one lays more emphasis on the importance of the learning process to technological development than E. F. Schumacher. He illustrates this by imagining a visit to a modern industrial refinery. He writes,

> "...As we walk around in its vastness,(...), we might well wonder how it was possible for the human mind to conceive such a thing. (...) How is it possible? The answer is that it did not spring ready-made out of any person's mind—it came by a process of evolution. (...) Least of all can we see the great educational background which is the precondition of all, (...) and without which nothing of what we actually see would be there. (...) . . . there is ten times as much somewhere else, which he cannot see, and without the ten, the one is worthless. And if the ten is not supplied by the country or society in which the refinery has been erected, either the refinery simply does

not work or it is, in fact, a foreign body depending for most of its life on some other society."[116]

The author defines development in terms of evolution rather than creation. If evolution is synonymous with development, then great attention has to be paid to the indigenous driving forces. Development would then involve the accumulation (not just the juxtaposition) of knowledge, techniques, and experiences that come with time, learning, and practice. However, this should not be construed as a call for a total rejection of all imported technology. For a long time to come, most developing countries will still have to import technology from the North. But it is high time they started initiating themselves into the practice of R&D.

For homemade technology to develop and flourish, there needs to be a market for it as well as for its products. The ability for local products to sell in a highly competitive market depends primarily on the attitude of consumers. At present, preference is for goods imported from the North, even where local products sell at more competitive prices. The problem here is one of value. People in the Third World tend to underrate homemade goods. Their motto is "Show me what you consume, and I'll tell the class in which you belong." The feeding bottle, considered a symbol of class distinction, is fast replacing the mother's breast. The very high cost of the former does not seem to discourage its use by today's nursing mothers in the Third World. Imported whisky, for instance, is preferred to local spirits extracted from banana or other products even though the latter may be just as good in quality and much more competitive in price. The same holds true for most other goods. A car assembled in Europe is preferred to another one of the same make produced under license in a Third World country.

There needs to be a change of attitude in the South in favor of homemade goods. This is one of the many conditions under which local

---

116   E. F. Schumacher, *Small Is Beautiful: A Study of Economics as if People Mattered* (London: ABACUS, 1974), 137-8.

production can be encouraged. It is up to governments in the South to create the atmosphere conducive to technological development. The choice here is between the prospects for self-sustained economic development and the present precarious one whose chances of success depend principally on outside factors. Indigenous entrepreneurs deserve the protection of their governments in conflicts that are likely to crop up between them and the powerful multinational companies.[117] Without such government support, the indigenous companies would be unable to find a footing in a market tightly controlled by the multinationals.

Experience in the developed countries has shown that even small firms are capable of great technological innovation. Governments in the developing countries must accept the responsibility of subsidizing research and development within private firms. They should also take upon themselves the payment of compensation for right of patent to local firms willing to diffuse their technology. Such technology could then be placed at the disposal of other indigenous entrepreneurs willing to use it.

There are usually no authorities responsible for defining the type of technology developed or imported. The entrepreneur or his representative is the sole arbiter in this respect. Laws relating to the import, the development, and the use of technology are almost always designed to guard against risks of physical danger to society and the environment or to ensure conformity with moral standards. Not much thought is ever given to the consequences of such decisions for labor or to the question of whether a certain type of technology will create jobs or, on the contrary, eliminate them. Very little consideration, if any, is given to their consequences on income distribution. For technology to qualify as appropriate, not only must it be adapted to and capable of assimilation by the recipient economy, but it must also be in keeping with the development objectives of that society. We may define these

---

117 Nicola Swainson, *The Development of Corporate Capitalism in Kenya: 1918-1977* (London: Heinemann, 1980), 270. One of such conflicts broke out between Bata Shoes and Tiger Shoe Co. of Kenya when the latter, an indigenous firm, tried to enter the local shoe market that was hitherto monopolized by the former.

objectives, broadly, as (a) raising the standard of living for all society, (b) raising employment level to its maximum, and (c) achieving relative economic autonomy.

Income levels will certainly rise with technical innovations. But to ensure an equitable distribution of the added wealth, steps should be taken to give all willing able-bodied persons the chance to make contributions to the creation of such wealth.

A lot depends on the choice of technology. Presented here below is a table showing the possible effects of imported technology on employment level with regard to the sources of raw materials and energy.

It is clear from the table that preference is to be given to capital-saving methods of production if the objective is to create jobs. The benefits, in terms of social gains, will be maximized if the imported technology calls for the use of local raw materials. The gains will be even greater in the case of the use of home-developed, labor-intensive technology. Much may thus be achieved if some effort is made to influence the type of technology developed or imported by society. Average ratios could be established for different sectors of the economy, and individual firms would, on their standing in relation to the relevant average, either pay a tax penalty or be granted a tax relief. For example, if a firm employs less labor than the average for the sector for a given quantity of fixed capital, it should be made to pay more taxes. If, on the contrary, the quantity of labor employed is greater than the established average for a given quantity of fixed capital, it should be granted tax cuts. Both the surtax and the reductions would be proportional to the difference observed between the capital-labor ratio for the firm and the established average ratio for that sector.

Similar measures could be taken to encourage the training of local labor in order to increase its productivity. There may be a chance here to reduce a country's dependence on expatriate staff.[118] Of course, the

---

118   Eventually, those using homemade capital goods would be exempted from paying any such surtax.

purpose is not to hinder technical progress but to make it evolve in the desired direction.[119]

Possible effects of imported technology on employment level with regard to changes in sources of raw materials.

	Imported labour-saving technology	Imported capital-saving technology
Source of raw materials energy unchanged	Low capacity to create jobs	High capacity to create jobs
Change to imported raw materials and energy	Negative capacity To create jobs	Capacity for jobs creation may be zero. For the total labour demand of the new procedures may be offset by those jobs lost in the change to imported raw materials and energy.
Change to local raw materials and energy	Capacity for job creation may be zero. For the loss of jobs resulting from the change to imported labour saving technology will be offset by other jobs created in the raw material sector.	Very high capacity for job creation. Labour demand will be high due to the labour intensive character of the technology and the labour needed to supply the raw materials and energy inputs.

Although it may prove most efficient if, to influence the evolution of technology, measures are taken at the international level, it is difficult to see how some nations (especially the technically advanced ones) can subscribe to such an arrangement. However, it is possible for a group of developing countries to agree to take joint steps aimed at minimizing the negative effects of technical progress. This would consist principally of selecting the type of technology they import or develop. Left alone, investor's decisions would continue to be influenced by their strong

119   *International Herald Tribune* (Paris), March 19, 1984, 3. Even in the North, not all technological innovations go unchallenged. For example, American farmworkers were, at one point, seeking to limit the right of research on farm mechanization that eliminated jobs. They claimed that thousands of jobs were being lost due to research on mechanical-harvesting systems and other devices.

penchant for profit. As long as they act within the law, nothing compels them to make concessions to society.

So far, investment in the Third World has mostly concentrated on the purchase of equipment for the manufacture of consumer goods. The argument for this is that by producing these goods at home, developing countries will be able to reduce their balance of payment deficits. This strategy has not really succeeded. What has happened is that there has been a partial shift from the import of consumer goods to that of capital goods without any reduction of the dependence of the LDCs on developed countries. Balance of payment problems have even aggravated. Investment in the production of capital goods has thus been maintained until recently at a very low level, if not entirely neglected. This, to say the least, has been a great error on the part of development planners in the South. It is high time that attention be paid to this all-important sector of the economy. As Jane Jacobs points out, *an economy that is not turning out for itself increasingly wide ranges of producers' goods is not making "large strides toward development," no matter what it is buying.*[120] The advantages involved are, indeed, enormous. Among other things, investing in the capital-goods sector at home would contribute to the learning process and would help in the formation of a skilled labor force. It would reduce a country's dependence on foreign technology. A successful capital-goods sector would also have a bearing on the balance of payments. As a country becomes capable of producing its own industrial equipment, the need to import such goods would be reduced. Another likely result of the establishment of a producer-goods sector in the developing countries would be a fall in the price of similar goods from the North. As the South increases its capacity to produce such goods, the North becomes more willing to settle for lower export prices. In other words, the terms of trade for this category of goods would gradually become less unfavorable to the South.

The effect of such a policy on employment might well be a favorable one. As the capital-goods sector develops, there would be increased

120   Jane Jacobs, *Cities and the Wealth of Nations* (New York: Random House, 1984), 139.

demand for labor. The result would be an increase in the Third World's share of the world output of producer goods.

Examples have been set by the ASEAN countries who have become not only self-sufficient but also net exporters of certain categories of capital goods.

Another major advantage in the production of producer goods at local levels is the low capital outlay required. This is true, at least for investment in the production of capital goods for small-scale industries. It surely costs less to produce equipment for family-sized soap-manufacturing units than it does to produce machines for a chemical complex.

The problem of capital shortage can thus be greatly reduced if local entrepreneurs are given the chance to invest in small projects.[121] This would allow for further reductions in the economy's dependence on foreign capital.

The development of a domestic producer-goods sector is a challenge open to both research institutions and the entrepreneur class in the Third World. Their governments should find ways and means of encouraging the production of capital goods at home. During the early stages, at least, of the development of such a sector, equipment would not be competitive on the international market. Investors might then show a preference for equipment from industrialized countries. Government policy would then be needed to make up for the disadvantages suffered by the domestic industry.

In a bid to encourage import-substitution industries, many Third World countries have had to raise trade barriers against certain classes of consumer goods. Simultaneously, they have granted tax reductions to importers of manufacturing equipment. Although these policies have been, to a certain extent, instrumental to the creation of the local

---

121   It is assumed here that the newly established capital-goods sector would not immediately undertake the production of very complex and thus expensive equipment. That is, they would start with the production of very simple capital goods that would be within the reach of the average indigenous entrepreneur.

consumer-goods industry, they have not in any way encouraged the formation of a capital-goods sector in these countries.

Production units for consumer goods have merely been transferred from the center to the periphery while the center has continued to exert effective control over production. This will be the case for as long as the periphery remains unable to produce its own capital goods. In order to encourage the local production of investment goods, governments in the South need to adopt policies similar to those that, in the '60s and the '70s, encouraged the local production of certain categories of consumer goods. Tax cuts should be granted to companies that invest in the capital-goods sector. Few foreign companies would be willing to invest in this sector, for as earlier observed, this would militate against their long-term interests, which lie in the preservation of their production secrets. Local entrepreneurs and governments in the South would have to be the prime movers of such an action.

The first commercial objective of such ventures would naturally be the domestic as well as the regional markets of which a country is a member. The manufacturer of small production units would first aim at covering the market for this product in his own area, then his country, then other countries in the region. It will be unrealistic to aim at the markets in developed countries from the very beginning, given the keen competition from established manufacturers and the huge capital investments involved. Many government-financed projects (the so-called prestige projects) have had to be scaled down or abandoned because the market estimates that determined the size of the investments were overoptimistic. A case in mind is that of CELUCAM, the wood pulp industrial complex in the south of Cameroon.

The ability of the poor to escape the effects of John K. Galbraith's "equilibrium of poverty" depends greatly on the encouragement they get from their government. Where adequate measures are taken to reduce uncertainty and the pressure of multinationals, small entrepreneurs can be expected to rise up and seek to improve their lot. Considering their limited capacity to save and their limited ability to assimilate technology, they should be given a chance to invest, first, in small industries involving very simple techniques. Home producers should be able to supply the market with such simple technology.

Efforts to incorporate local resources into production should not in any way be limited to the manufacturing sector. These resources should also be used, in a generally profitable way, in the provision of certain items of social overhead capital. Acute shortages of capital goods may be partially made up for by substituting available manpower for certain categories of machinery. Unused, cheap labor could, indeed, be a great asset. The lack of good roads in most Third World countries greatly hinders the circulation of goods and people. While it is costly to import earthmoving equipment for road construction, the unemployed labor force could serve as a suitable substitute. Many of the roads that existed in Africa before independence were constructed with human labor, not with the heavy equipment of today. So were most hospitals and schools. The importation of machinery was minimal at the time. Today, most roads, even in the least-developed countries, are constructed with the aid of very heavy equipment, which reduces the demand of local labor to the bare minimum. This means draining the countries of the South of their foreign reserves, given that they have to import these machines. On balance, using local manpower in the place of certain categories of imported machineries could be advantageous to the economy. For while the imported machineries engender an outflow of resources, the employment of the local workforce does not directly cause any such outflow. The income so earned by the workers may, through the multiplier principle, stimulate the local economy. This would, however, depend on the economy's ability to produce those goods that this class of income earners is likely to consume. By employing local labor and other resources, a country would be contributing to efforts aimed at achieving some of its development objectives. It would be providing jobs for the unemployed and giving the chance for them to improve their income levels. The economy, as a whole, would be reducing its dependence on external factors.

POSTSCRIPT

However much the Northern countries may want development in the South, they want the preservation of their privileges even more. The continued absence of development in the South is, in part, the result of this preference for the preservation of acquired privileges, the preference for security, and the rejection of the risk inherent in the eventual development in the South. The Northern economies are at present sagging under overcapacity, yet the transfer of some of their surplus resources that can help transform the South is, from their point of view, irrational or inappropriate. For too long, we have been made to believe that the poor countries can develop only by imitating the developed ones. Escape through other means is made even more difficult by the impression given that all is being done in the North to bring relief. That, by granting aid, the developed countries deliberately seek to maintain the LDCs in the state of perpetual underdevelopment (which would be tantamount to sabotage), is yet to be clearly shown. But that, a substantial part of such aid produces just this effect, can hardly be gainsaid.

The poor countries of the South are made to borrow in order to finance the acquisition of capital goods and technology necessary to augment their productive capacities. But the conditions under which these are obtained and the price of the capital goods they import militate against capital formation. What was originally intended as a solution to their problem of capital shortage has become an additional problem. They have to pay back not only the funds they borrow but also huge interests on these loans. No wonder, therefore, that net income in these countries cannot increase beyond the subsistence level. No wonder that capital formation is almost impossible. The system is a vicious circle, comparable only to peonage.

Development along present lines does not appear to hold any promise for the Third World. Its chances of success are virtually nonexistent. This is so because it will hurt those on whom it depends for success. Moreover, insisting on developing along present lines will only set the countries of the South on a collision course with those of the North who, out of self-interest imperatives, will normally be opposed to such development.

All development that is propelled from without is alien and, as such, will be short-lived. And again, as Jane Jacobs puts it, "Development is a do-it-yourself process; for any economy, it is either do it yourself or don't develop."

People in the South must come to terms with that reality. They must recognize the fact that there are no shortcuts to development. Genuine development will be instigated only from within. Outside assistance may only quicken the pace of development; it will not initiate it. The developed countries should not be counted upon to bring development to the South. They will not do it. They have their own axes to grind and their own interests to protect. And these are not always compatible with those of the South. Often, they conflict with them.

The problem posed by uncontrolled population growth in the Third World ought to be taken very seriously. It obviously obstructs economic progress by not allowing for capital formation. Medical science has contributed much to the reduction in child mortality. But in the absence of measures to control birth rates, there is bound to be overpopulation at some point. Given the productive capacities of most Third World countries, it can be said that many of them are overpopulated. Widespread poverty and famine are only the most visible characteristics of this overpopulation.

A maxim popular with people of the Ejagham tribe runs thus: *If you add a child, you must add a mound.*[122] In other words, as a new baby is born into the family, the farmland under cultivation must be increased. However, the burdens of child upbringing go far beyond those of providing him or her with food. All the same, the maxim still holds true. It is economically unwise for the population to grow uncontrollably without a corresponding growth in society's available economic resources. Where the increase in these resources is difficult to obtain, birth control ought to be encouraged.

Without questioning the standard of education in most schools and universities in the Third World, it should be admitted, however, that their curricula do not reflect the specific needs of their societies. Most of those who graduate there in engineering, for instance, are not prepared for the type of problems they are likely to encounter in real life. With the exception of a few universities and research centers that are closely involved in work on appropriate technology, many engineering schools in the South still prepare their students for work in industries designed to suit the needs of developed countries. The result is the ever-growing gap between the knowledge available and that needed to solve the problems of the vast majority of people in the Third World.

Should the South just adopt and apply economic theories handed down from the North without any questioning? The answer, certainly, is no. Economic theorists like Adam Smith and David Ricardo were people too. So they too had interests to promote. At least, the society or the nation in which they belonged and whose sympathies they shared had interests worth defending. As much as they could, they protected and promoted the interests of that society—to which they were more or less beholden. It would have been unthinkable that they would formulate and promote economic theories that were good for the rest of the world (or for any part thereof) but bad for their home country, England. On the other hand, it is possible that they did espouse policies that were

122   The Ejagham are an ethnic group in the Manyu Division in the southwest region of Cameroon.

favorable to England, irrespective of the effect of such policies on other nations. That would be consistent with the logic of self-interest. The problem is that the rest of the world, especially the South, adopted, almost without questioning, ideas that were formulated with the interests of a particular part of the world in mind. Perhaps, people in the South ought to share John Maynard Keynes's skepticism regarding the power of ideas that he thinks is more than that of vested interests. He says, *"Soon or late, it is ideas, not vested interest, which are dangerous for good or evil."*[123] The question now is, What if the power of ideas that Keynes considers *'dangerous for good or evil'* is used to support and promote vested interests that, by definition, are susceptible to being biased? David Ricardo's international trade theory appears to be the result of such a combination of vested interests (the national interests of England, his country) and the power of "dangerous ideas." And today, we all know what we got for embracing and adopting those ideas: a situation where, as Erik Reinert puts it, *"one part of the international community has specialized in being rich, while the other is specializing in being poor."*

---

123   John M. Keynes, *General Theory of Employment* (BN Publishing, 2008), last sentence in the book.

INDEX OF WORDS AND NAMES